First published by Parragon in 2009

Parragon
Queen Street House
4 Queen Street
Bath BA1 1HE, UK

TheFA.com

Produced by Parragon under licence by The Football Association Ltd.
All information correct at time of creation, April 2009
All photography © PA Photos

ISBN 978-1-84535-408-4

Printed in China

ENGLAND

THE OFFICIAL ENGLAND ANNUAL 2010

Parragon

Bath New York Singapore Hong Kong Cologne Delhi Melbourne

MATTHEW UPSON

Upson's **impressive performances** with previous club Birmingham City led to his international call-up in May 2003 to face South Africa. In 2008, he firmly established his place at the heart of England's defence, featuring in the last four internationals of the year. Upson scored his first international goal against Germany in November 2008.

BORN 18.04.79, Hartismere
POSITION Defender
CLUB West Ham United
CAPS 14
ENGLAND DEBUT 22.05.03, against South Africa

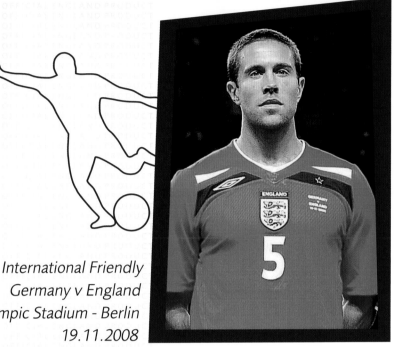

International Friendly
Germany v England
Olympic Stadium - Berlin
19.11.2008

GARETH BARRY

When Gareth Barry played against Spain in 2007, it was his first international appearance in four years. Since then, Barry has played in 20 consecutive matches for his country and is yet to miss a game under Fabio Capello. The Aston Villa midfielder grabbed his first England goal in 2008, to go with the ten caps he earned that same year.

BORN 23.02.81, Hastings
POSITION Midfielder
CLUB Aston Villa
CAPS 29
ENGLAND DEBUT 31.05.00, against Ukraine

World Cup 2010
Qualifying Round Group 6
England v Ukraine
Wembley Stadium - London
01.04.2009

BORN 22.07.84, Middlesbrough
POSITION Midfielder
CLUB Middlesbrough
CAPS 23
ENGLAND DEBUT 09.02.05, against Holland

Having earned seven England Under-21 caps, Downing was called up for the senior squad to face Holland in 2005. Displaying **pace** and **top-class crossing** ability, Fabio Capello became the third successive England manager to give Downing an England cap, in a 1-0 friendly defeat to France in March 2008.

World Cup 2010
Qualifying Round Group 6
Andorra v England
Olympic Stadium - Barcelona
06.09.2008

STEWART DOWNING

PROFILES

MICHAEL CARRICK

Carrick's performances with previous club sides Tottenham Hotspur and West Ham United led to an England recall for England's tour of the USA in May 2005. He was named in the Three Lions squad by Fabio Capello for the first time in August 2008.

International Friendly
Germany v England
Olympic Stadium - Berlin
19.11.2008

BORN 28.07.81, Wallsend
POSITION Midfielder
CLUB Manchester United
CAPS 17
ENGLAND DEBUT 25.05.01, against Mexico

England have never won the European Championship, initially called the **'European Nations Cup'**, but have twice reached the semi-final stage. Off to a bumpy start, England didn't enter the first tournament in 1960 and lost 6-3 on aggregate to France in the Preliminary Round of the next. **Fortunes turned in 1968 when Sir Alf Ramsey guided England to a 2-0 victory against USSR in the match for third place** - Bobby Charlton and Geoff Hurst scoring. England lost out on a place in the Finals after a bruising semi in Florence against Yugoslavia in which Alan Mullery became the first England player in history to be sent off.

West Germany were by far the strongest team in Europe in 1972 and the eventual winners of the tournament, so it was no surprise they beat England 3-1 on aggregate in the Quarter-finals. England's campaign to qualify for the next Championship...**got off to the perfect start in Yugoslavia '76 as the Three**

Lions beat the Czechs, ultimately European Champions, 3-0 at Wembley. England also triumphed 5-0 against Cyprus. Still England failed to qualify. Ron Greenwood's team did make it to the Group Finals of 1980, but a 1-0 defeat to the Italian hosts ended England's hopes.

European Championship Final
West Germany v USSR
18.06.1972

Three disappointing tournaments followed for England. After failing to qualify in 1984, England disastrously lost all three First Round matches in the 1988 Finals in West Germany, and didn't progress beyond the First Round again in the Swedish Finals of 1992.

Malcolm Macdonald soars in with his fourth goal during the European Championship qualifying match at Wembley Stadium. England won 5-0, and Malcolm Macdonald scored the lot. 16.04.1975

England hosted a brilliant Championship in 1996 that will be remembered for the drama of its penalty shootouts. Terry Venables' team won 2-0 against Scotland and 4-1 against Holland before Alan Shearer's early goal in the semi-final with Germany. The Germans equalised and England finally bowed out on penalties after a thrilling period of extra-time.

There was another First Round exit in 2000, though **England did beat Germany for the first time for 34 years in a competitive match**. **England reached the quarter-final stage in Portugal in 2004** and may have gone further if **Wayne Rooney, then just 18, hadn't been injured against the hosts**. With only a point needed from England's last Euro 2008 qualifier at home to Croatia, Peter Crouch's volley made it 2-2 with 25 minutes to go. But the Wembley crowd was stunned into silence as Petric knocked the home side out of the competition with an angled drive.

ENGLAND HOSTED A BRILLIANT CHAMPIONSHIP IN 1996

England's Alan Shearer celebrates after scoring his side's goal in their European Championship semi-final against Germany at Wembley 26.06.1996

EUROPEAN CHAMPIONSHIP PERFORMANCES

YEAR	HOSTS	ENGLAND'S PERFORMANCE	WINNERS
1960	France	Did not enter	USSR
1964	Spain	Did not qualify	Spain
1968	Italy	Semi-finals	Italy
1972	Belgium	Quarter-finals*	West Germany
1976	Yugoslavia	Did not qualify	Czechoslovakia
1980	Italy	Round 1	West Germany
1984	France	Did not qualify	France
1988	West Germany	Round 1	Holland
1992	Sweden	Round 1	Denmark
1996	England	Semi-finals	Germany
2000	Belgium & Holland	Round 1	France
2004	Portugal	Quarter-finals	Greece
2008	Austria & Switzerland	Did not qualify	Spain

*The quarter-finals weren't part of the Belgian finals

GUESS WHO

CLUB SIDE IS MANCHESTER UNITED

FIRST NAME HAS SEVEN LETTERS

SECOND NAME HAS SEVEN LETTERS

FIRST NAME STARTS WITH M

SECOND NAME STARTS WITH C

PLAYS IN MIDFIELD

Answer:

Answer: Michael Carrick.

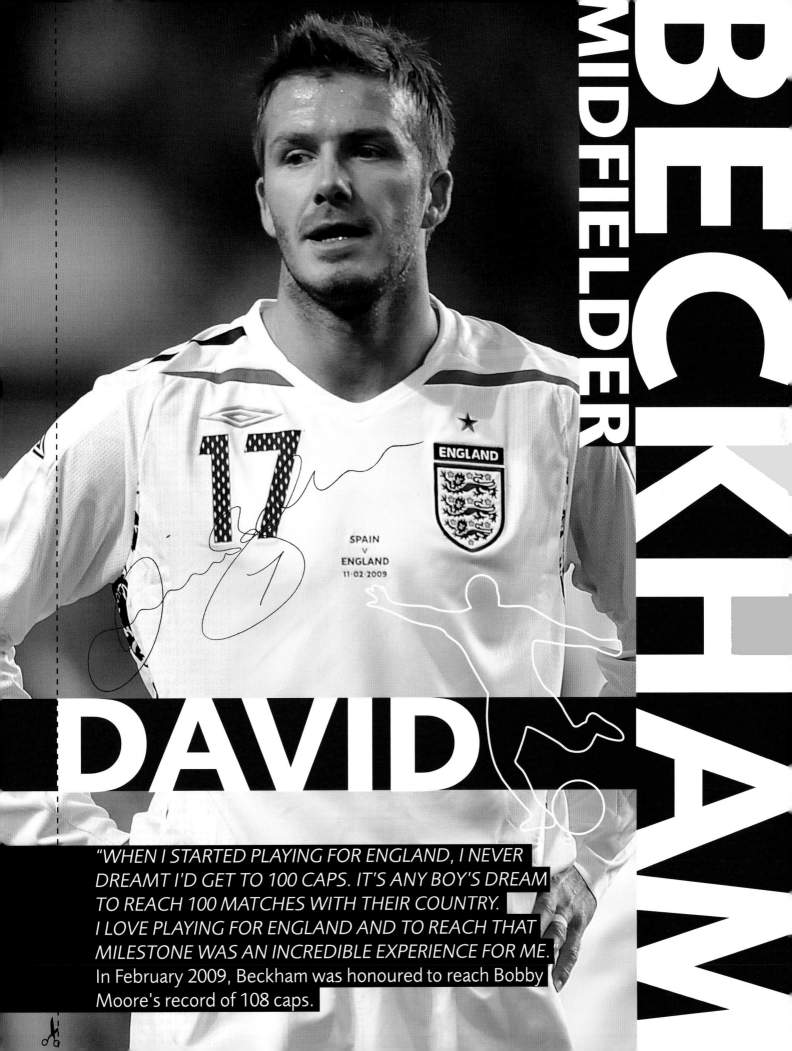

BECKHAM
MIDFIELDER

DAVID

"WHEN I STARTED PLAYING FOR ENGLAND, I NEVER DREAMT I'D GET TO 100 CAPS. IT'S ANY BOY'S DREAM TO REACH 100 MATCHES WITH THEIR COUNTRY. I LOVE PLAYING FOR ENGLAND AND TO REACH THAT MILESTONE WAS AN INCREDIBLE EXPERIENCE FOR ME." In February 2009, Beckham was honoured to reach Bobby Moore's record of 108 caps.

GOALKEEPER
DAVID JAMES

In the past few years, David James has re-established himself as one of the best goalkeepers in England and ultimately earned himself a recall to the national side.

"I ALWAYS WANT TO BE INVOLVED WITH ENGLAND AND WOULDN'T RETIRE FROM IT. IF THE NEW MANAGER FANCIES IT THEN IT WOULD BE NICE TO BE IN THE FRAME. I WASN'T UNHAPPY WITH MY FORM FOR MY CLUB AND WASN'T TRAINING BADLY FOR ENGLAND SO THERE WASN'T AN OBVIOUS REASON FOR NOT BEING INVOLVED."

FOOTY SKILLS WORDSEARCH

FIND ALL THE FOOTY SKILLS AND TECHNIQUES IN THE GRID BELOW.

DRIBBLING	DRAG BACK	HEADING
CUSHION CONTROL	DEFENDING	SET PIECES
SHOOTING	BLOCK TACKLE	PENALTIES
HOOK TURN	SLIDE TACKLE	FREE KICK
FEINTING	JOCKEYING	SHOT STOPPING

```
G G D R I B B L I N G C V P S
W S H O O T I N G O F U D E H
H O O K T U R N O T R S H N O
B L O C K T A C K L E H R A T
L S W N H U U Z V B E I T L S
E E L Q G E Q X V W K O J T T
Y G Q I D E F E N D I N G I O
W H V P D A F C E V C C R E P
J A P I W E U G L H K O S S P
W O G M U H T L T D E N Z W I
V H D R A G B A C K E T A L N
F E I N T I N G C Q M R V L G
M F H E A D I N G K D O K I J
T J O C K E Y I N G L L M I S
F S E T P I E C E S Z E I N X
```

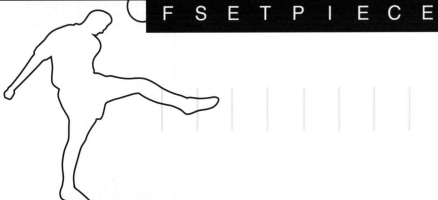

Answers:

BORN 09.07.85, Stevenage
POSITION Forward
CLUB Aston Villa
CAPS 4

Ashley Young was given his first England cap by Steve McClaren, when he came on as a substitute in the Vienna friendly against Austria in November 2007. Young went on to feature in three more England internationals in 2008, as a substitute. His continuing good form at club level proves he could be part of the England scene for a long time.

"HE MAKES THINGS HAPPEN. THERE IS AN EXPECTATION NOW OVER HIM, NOT JUST FROM MYSELF BUT HIS COLLEAGUES AND THE CROWD. HE IS TERRIFIC."
Martin O'Neill, Aston Villa manager

INTERNATIONAL FRIENDLY
ENGLAND V SWITZERLAND
WEMBLEY STADIUM - LONDON
06.02.2008

ASHLEY YOUNG

CARLTON COLE:

Cole started the 2008-09 season in **good form**, scoring four goals in his first eight games for his Premier League club, West Ham United. Cole received his first senior England call up for an international friendly against Spain in February 2009. Entering the match in the 75th minute as a substitute, he almost levelled the scores as he **flashed a half-volley** over the bar.

BORN 12.10.83, Croydon
POSITION Striker
CLUB West Ham
CAPS 2

"CARLTON IS GETTING BETTER AND BETTER, AND FOR ME IS NOT YET AT HIS PEAK. SOMETIMES WHEN HE IS HOLDING THE BALL, HE REMINDS ME OF MARK HUGHES. HUGHES WAS FANTASTIC AT HOLDING AND PROTECTING THE BALL. CARLTON IS CLOSE TO HIM, BUT ALSO VERY FAST."
Gianfranco Zola, West Ham United manager

INTERNATIONAL FRIENDLY
SPAIN V ENGLAND
RAMON SANCHEZ-PIZJUAN STADIUM - SEVILLE
11.02.2009

The First Team

The England national team was once made up of amateurs, the **first official international match being played against Scotland** at the West of Scotland Cricket Club at Partick, near Glasgow, on 30 November 1872.

The game ended in a 0-0 draw but a tradition had been set in motion and it was not long before Wales and Ireland were added to England's international fixture card.

FIRST OFFICIAL INTERNATIONAL MATCH PLAYED AGAINST SCOTLAND

The **England team has always been run by The Football Association**, Charles Alcock, Secretary of The FA between 1870 and 1895, becoming the driving force behind establishing an England team in 1870.

Belgium, in 1923, were the first European side to play a full international in England, and a year later England played their first match at Wembley Stadium, drawing 1-1 with Scotland (although it was not to become England's permanent home until 1966).

*World Cup Switzerland 1954
Quarter-final - England v Uruguay.
England's Billy Wright (second l) clears up an attack, watched by team-mate Bill McGarry (second r) and Uruguay's Oscar Miguez (l) and Julio Cesar Abbadie (r)*

ENGLAND

In 1899, a Football Association side toured Germany, but it was in **1908 that the full England team went on its first overseas tour**, to Austria, Hungary and Bohemia (as the Czech Republic was then called), England winning all four games.

It was in 1929 that England lost for the first time to European opponents when Spain triumphed 4-3 in Madrid. More remarkable though, is the fact that it was not until 1953, **81 years after the first international, that England lost at home to a national side from continental Europe – Hungary winning 6-3**.

After a disagreement with FIFA over payments to amateur players, England did not enter the World Cups in 1930, 1934 and 1938.

After the Second World War, England rejoined FIFA and duly entered the World Cup in 1950, hosted by Brazil. England, hampered by climatic conditions, failed to progress beyond their first round group.

In the 1954 World Cup in Switzerland, England fared better, losing in the quarter-finals to Uruguay. Four years later, England drew all their group games and failed to qualify for the knock-out phase. In 1962, England progressed to the quarter-finals where they were beaten by Brazil.

ENGLAND WORLD CUP 1966

England's captain Bobby Moore, carried shoulder high by his team-mates, holds aloft the FIFA World Cup, July 30, 1966. England defeated West Germany 4-2 in the final, played at London's Wembley Stadium. From left to right, goalkeeper Gordon Banks (partially obscured), Alan Ball, Martin Peters, Geoff Hurst, Bobby Moore, Ray Wilson, George Cohen and Bobby Charlton.

HISTORY

England's finest international hour came four years later in 1966, when Bobby Moore lifted the Jules Rimet trophy at Wembley on 30 July.

Grouped with Uruguay, Mexico and France, England drew one game and won the others to progress to the quarter-finals where Argentina lay in wait. England won a bruising encounter 1-0 and then beat Portugal 2-1 in the semis.

In the final, **England won 4-2 after extra-time, with Geoff Hurst scoring a hat-trick**, the only man to do so in a World Cup Final. The team that day was: G Banks, G Cohen, R Wilson, N Stiles, J Charlton, R Moore, A Ball, R Hunt, R Charlton, G Hurst, M Peters.

England's next-best performance at a World Cup was in 1990 when losing to West Germany on penalties in the Semi-final.

England first entered the then European Nations Cup in 1962/63, losing in the first round to France. In 1968, England fared better, getting to the semi-finals, a feat they repeated in 1996.

Over 1,100 players have been selected for England's senior team, with Peter Shilton, on 125 appearances, the most capped player. Bobby Charlton, with 49 goals, is England's leading goal-scorer.

*World Cup Italia 1990
Semi-final
West Germany v England
Stadio Delle Alpi.
England's Paul Gascoigne
(second r) lashes a shot past
West Germany's Andreas
Brehme (r) as team mate Mark
Wright (c) and Germany's
Rudi Voller (l) and Bodo Illgner
(second l) look on.*

ENGLAND

OVER 1,100 PLAYERS HAVE BEEN SELECTED FOR ENGLAND'S SENIOR TEAM

England also entered the UEFA European Football Championship (formerly the European Nations Cup).

Following the arrival of Sven-Goran Eriksson as Head Coach in January 2001, the England team enjoyed a period of inspired form, recording five successive World Cup victories against Finland, Albania (twice), Greece and Germany, before securing dramatic qualification for the World Cup Finals in Asia, with captain David Beckham's last minute equaliser against Greece.

During the 2002 World Cup in South Korea and Japan, England qualified from the 'group of death' recording a memorable victory over Argentina in the Sapporo Dome. A 3-0 win against Denmark in the pouring rain set up a quarter-final against Brazil, where Michael Owen gave the Three Lions great hope when he opened the scoring early on.

PETER SHILTON, 125 APPEARANCES FOR ENGLAND

In their last World Cup, in Germany, there was heartbreak as Portugal knocked England out of the competition on penalties at the Quarter-final stage. After a 0-0 draw in Gelsenkirchen, the Three Lions, who had been reduced to 10 men following the dismissal of Wayne Rooney, once again failed from 12 yards.

Manchester United's Cristiano Ronaldo scored the all-important goal after Frank Lampard, Jamie Carragher and Steven Gerrard had all missed.

That game marked Eriksson's last in charge and new Head Coach Steve McClaren took over as England looked towards their Euro 2008 qualification campaign.

Steve McClaren was in charge of the Three Lions for 18 games, winning nine, but after missing out on qualification for Euro 2008 his contract was terminated on 22 November 2007.

HISTORY

However, goals from Rivaldo and Ronaldinho sent England home and crushed their hopes of lifting the world's biggest prize.

On Friday 14 December 2007, The FA confirmed the appointment of **Fabio Capello as the new England Manager. He started his job at Soho Square on 7 January 2008, with qualification for the 2010 World Cup in South Africa his initial objective.**

DAVID JAMES

BORN 01.08.70, Welwyn Garden City
POSITION Goalkeeper
CLUB Portsmouth
CAPS 48
ENGLAND DEBUT 29.03.97, against Mexico

James won his first senior England cap against Mexico in 1997 and his excellent goalkeeping skills helped England qualify for Euro 2004. In April 2007 James **broke the record for the most clean sheets** in Premier League history. As of 14 February 2009, James achieved the all-time Premier League record of **536 appearances**.

International Friendly
England v USA
Wembley Stadium - London
28.05.2008

PLAYER

With his **electric pace** and **attacking instinct**, Cole was an ever-present for England in the 2002 World Cup, Euro 2004 and 2006 World Cup. Cole has played a crucial role in England's start to the 2010 World Cup qualification campaign, playing every minute of the first three wins of Group Six.

BORN 20.12.80, Stepney
POSITION Left back
CLUB Chelsea
CAPS 71
ENGLAND DEBUT 28.03.01, against Albania

World Cup 2010
Qualifying Round Group 6
England v Ukraine
Wembley Stadium - London
01.04.2009

ASHLEY COLE

RIO FERDINAND

BORN 07.11.78, Peckham
POSITION Defender
CLUB Manchester United
CAPS 73
ENGLAND DEBUT 15.11.97, against Cameroon

Ferdinand's commanding performances for England in the 2002 World Cup cemented his status as one of the world's best defenders. He made eight England appearances throughout 2008 and **captained his country on three occasions**. Ahead of the friendly against Czech Republic in August 2008, he was named England's **vice captain**.

World Cup 2010
Qualifying Round Group 6
England v Ukraine
Wembley Stadium - London
01.04.2009

PROFILES

JOHN TERRY

As captain of one of Europe's most powerful club sides, Terry is known as one of the world's most respected defenders. His **leadership** qualities impressed Fabio Capello, who named him **permanent captain** in August 2008. Terry successfully led England to victory in their opening two World Cup qualifiers, including a 4-1 victory over Croatia.

BORN 07.12.80, Barking
POSITION Defender
CLUB Chelsea
CAPS 51
ENGLAND DEBUT 03.06.03, against Serbia & Montenegro

World Cup 2010
Qualifying Round Group 6
Andorra v England
Olympic Stadium - Barcelona
06.09.2008

23

STANLEY MATTHEWS

WINGER   1934-57   54 CAPS   11 GOALS

The legendary Stanley Matthews was known as the **Wizard of Dribble**, with his trademark style of moving around the pitch with the ball seemingly glued to his feet. His skills ensured he became **England's first Footballer of the Year** in 1948 and European Footballer of the Year in 1956.

His Blackpool team seemed doomed to fail in the 1953 FA Cup Final against Bolton. But in an amazing fightback, Matthews' style was in full force and helped his team secure a fantastic 4-3 victory. The match was famously dubbed the **'Matthews Final'**.

ENGLAND

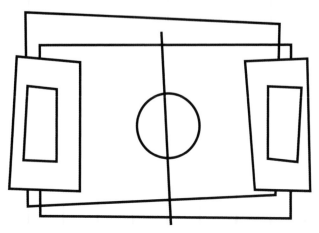

Matthews played 54 times for England between the ages of 19 and 42. He became his **country's oldest international** against Denmark in 1957.

JIMMY GREAVES

STRIKER   1959-67   57 CAPS   44 GOALS

INTERNATIONAL FRIENDLY
ENGLAND V HUNGARY
05.05.1965

Jimmy Greaves was the most **prolific goalscorer** and one of the most lethal strikers in the world. He was famous for scoring on his debuts and scored England's only goal in his first national team appearance against Peru in 1959.

In his club career, Greaves scored **357 top-flight goals**, including three **five-goal hauls**, and scored on his debut for every club he played for.

LEGENDS

When playing for Tottenham, he scored **37 League goals** in just **41 matches**, still a club record today.

A legendary marksman, Greaves scored the first of **six England hat-tricks when he was 20**, when Luxembourg were beaten 9-0 in a World Cup qualifier. His **hat-trick record** still stands to this day.

IDENTIFY THE PLAYER

CAN YOU WORK OUT WHO THE MIXED-UP PLAYERS ARE?

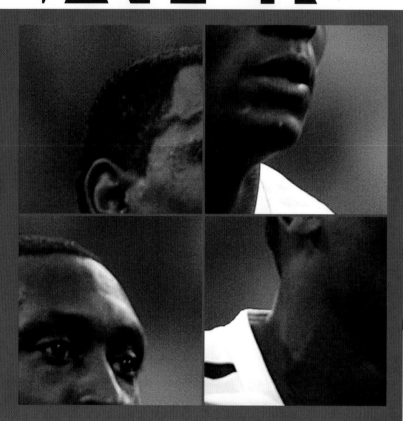

Answer:

Answer:

Answers: top left, Emile Heskey and bottom right, David Beckham.

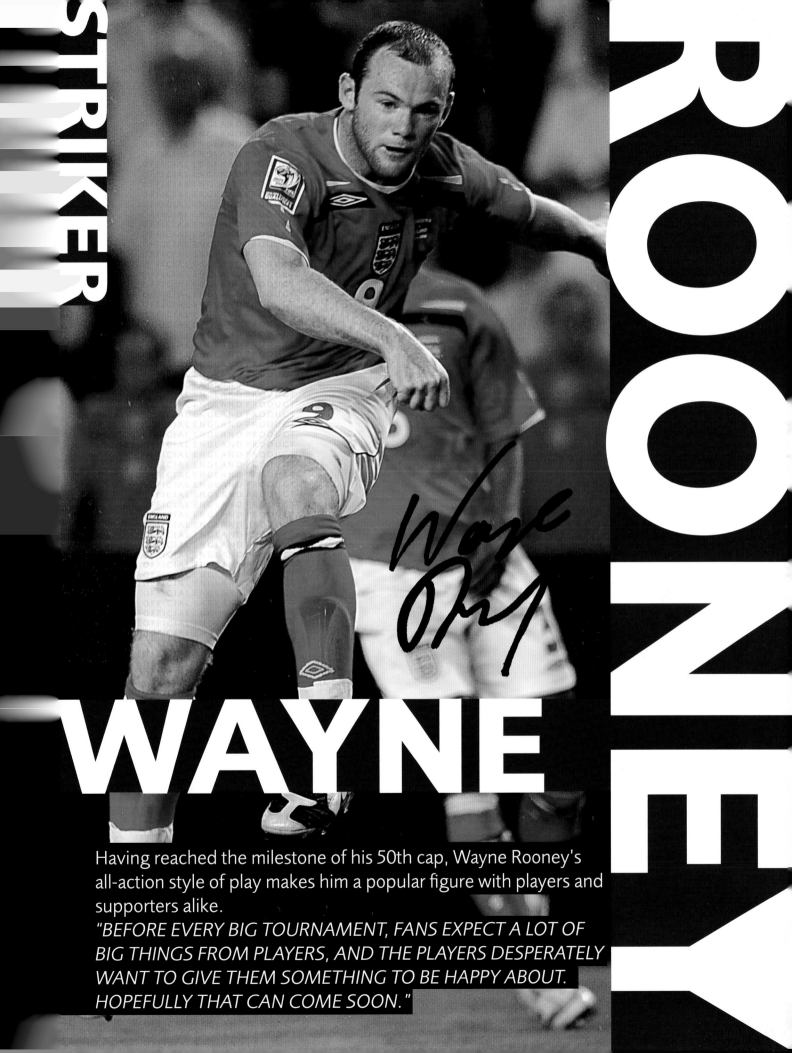

STRIKER

WAYNE ROONEY

Having reached the milestone of his 50th cap, Wayne Rooney's all-action style of play makes him a popular figure with players and supporters alike.

"BEFORE EVERY BIG TOURNAMENT, FANS EXPECT A LOT OF BIG THINGS FROM PLAYERS, AND THE PLAYERS DESPERATELY WANT TO GIVE THEM SOMETHING TO BE HAPPY ABOUT. HOPEFULLY THAT CAN COME SOON."

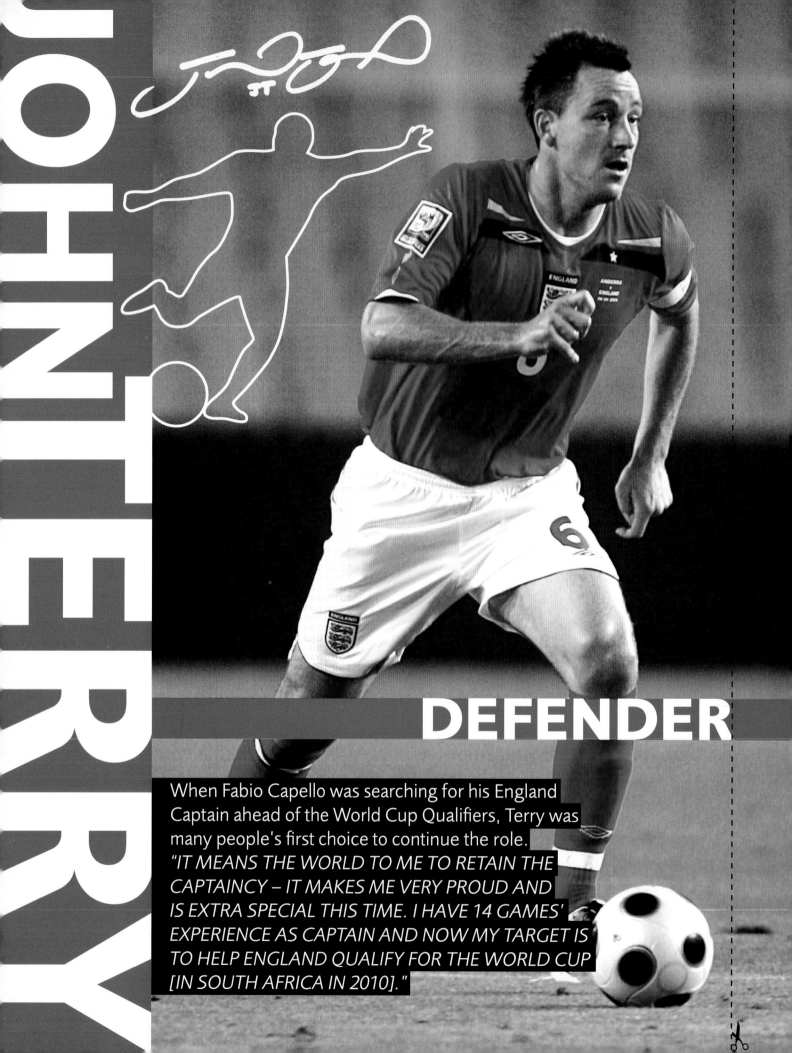

JOHN TERRY

DEFENDER

When Fabio Capello was searching for his England Captain ahead of the World Cup Qualifiers, Terry was many people's first choice to continue the role. *"IT MEANS THE WORLD TO ME TO RETAIN THE CAPTAINCY – IT MAKES ME VERY PROUD AND IS EXTRA SPECIAL THIS TIME. I HAVE 14 GAMES' EXPERIENCE AS CAPTAIN AND NOW MY TARGET IS TO HELP ENGLAND QUALIFY FOR THE WORLD CUP [IN SOUTH AFRICA IN 2010]."*

UNRAVEL THE MIXED-UP WORDS TO REVEAL THE OTHER TEAMS IN ENGLAND'S 2010 WORLD CUP QUALIFYING GROUP.

DORARNA

‒ ‒ ‒ ‒ ‒ ‒ ‒

TARIOCA

‒ ‒ ‒ ‒ ‒ ‒ ‒

LABURES

‒ ‒ ‒ ‒ ‒ ‒ ‒

TAZKAKSHNA

‒ ‒ ‒ ‒ ‒ ‒ ‒ ‒ ‒ ‒

KUREINA

‒ ‒ ‒ ‒ ‒ ‒ ‒

Answers: Andorra, Croatia, Belarus, Kazakhstan and Ukraine.

ARGENTINA

England's 13 matches with Argentina have included five in the World Cup, four Wembley friendlies and one in Buenos Aires that was abandoned when the pitch flooded and became a lake!

Alf Ramsey's **England faced the favourites Argentina in the Quarter-finals of the 1966 World Cup**. From the first attack, it was clear that the South Americans were determined to stop England at all costs.

World Cup Quarter-final match in Mexico. Argentina's Diego Maradona appears to handle the ball to score the opening goal. 22.06.1986

England's meeting with Argentina at the Mexico World Cup in 1986 was another electrifying match. The match sprang to life five minutes into the second period, Steve Hodge flicking a looping back-pass towards Peter Shilton. **The subsequent clash saw Diego Maradona make his infamous 'Hand of God' goal, which the referee incredibly allowed to stand.**

GREAT

Visiting **captain Antonio Rattin was sent off by the referee for persistent dissent, and play was held up for seven minutes as Rattin asked for an interpreter before eventually leaving the field**. Geoff Hurst headed the only goal from Peters' superb cross and ill feeling was so strong by the end, that the traditional shirt-swapping didn't take place.

Four minutes later Maradona collected the ball just inside his own half and skipped past three hefty challenges before rifling home the goal of the tournament. Gary Lineker gave England hope with nine minutes left, but then missed when it seemed easier to score. England were out!

England again faced Argentina in the Second Round of the 1998 World Cup in France. The Argentinians scored with a penalty after five minutes, then England hit back to lead 2-1 with Alan Shearer's penalty and a wonderful Michael Owen goal that catapulted the 18-year-old to world stardom.

It was 2-2 at the break and a kick on Simeone saw David Beckham sent off, Sol Campbell had a goal disallowed and England finally went out on penalties. **There could hardly have been more drama**.

England got their revenge at the next World Cup in the Far East. When the teams clashed in the second group fixture in Sapporo, **Beckham's nerveless penalty after Pochettino's foul on Owen in the 44th minute being enough to secure the points**.

THERE COULD HARDLY HAVE BEEN MORE DRAMA.

RIVA

David Beckham scores from the penalty mark during the 2002 World Cup, Group F match against Argentina at the Sapporo Dome, Japan 07.06.2002

JOE HART

BORN 19.4.87, Shrewsbury
POSITION Goalkeeper
CLUB Manchester City
CAPS 1

At only 21 years and 43 days old and after 12 appearances at Under-21 level, Manchester City goalkeeper Joe Hart made his **debut** for the England senior team. Hart was a second-half substitute for David James in England's friendly against Trinidad & Tobago in June 2008, where he earned his **first senior cap**.

INTERNATIONAL FRIENDLY
TRINIDAD & TOBAGO V ENGLAND
HASELY CRAWFORD STADIUM
PORT OF SPAIN
01.06.2008

"IT'S GOOD TO GET THE NOD TO BE INVOLVED, BUT I WON'T TAKE ANYTHING FOR GRANTED. I KNOW FOR A FACT THAT COME THE NEXT SQUAD, I'M NOT DEFINITELY IN IT SO I'VE GOT TO KEEP WORKING HARD AND IF I DO GET A CHANCE TO SHOW WHAT I CAN DO. HOPEFULLY I'LL TAKE IT."

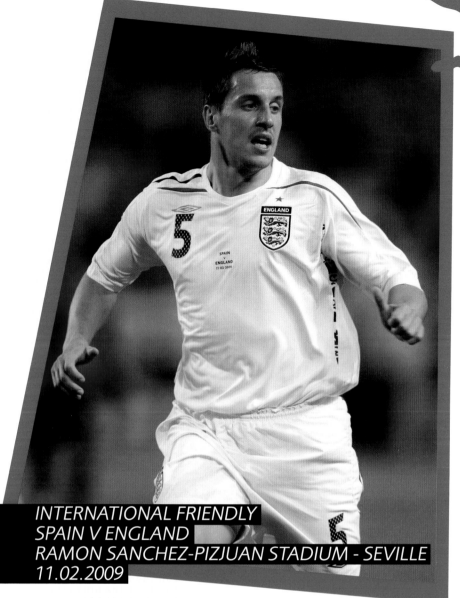

BORN 17.8.82, Manchester
POSITION Defender
CLUB Everton
CAPS 3

INTERNATIONAL FRIENDLY
SPAIN V ENGLAND
RAMON SANCHEZ-PIZJUAN STADIUM - SEVILLE
11.02.2009

Phil Jagielka made his first appearance for the England senior team in 2008, as England faced Trinidad & Tobago in June. Jagielka earned his first England cap as he came on as a second half sub in Port of Spain. Having had ambitions for **various roles** on the pitch, the Everton defender believes that playing consistently in the same position has enabled him to **excel** for his club side and he earned another international call against Spain in February 2009.

PHIL JAGIELKA

"MY DEBUT IN TRINIDAD WAS A BRILLIANT MOMENT, ESPECIALLY TO GET HALF A GAME AS WELL. IT WASN'T JUST FIVE MINUTES ON THE PITCH. IT WAS FANTASTIC AND SOMETHING I'VE ALWAYS WANTED TO DO."

Gary Lineker, an England legend with 48 goals in 80 internationals, once said: *"Football's a simple game. Twenty-two men chase after the ball and at the end the Germans win"*. Well, that's not strictly true. **England beat West Germany nine times, twice when they were the reigning World Champions,** and the unified Germany twice.

The English hosts had six consecutive victories against Germany under their belts when the two teams squared up that unforgettable July afternoon at Wembley for the World Cup Final of 1966.

World Cup England 1966 - England v West Germany Wembley - London. England's Nobby Stiles breaks away from West Germany's Siggi Held as England's George Cohen and Alan Ball look on. 30.07.1966

GREAT

After a tentative first few minutes, Haller pounced to put West Germany in front. Six minutes later **Bobby Moore, England's great captain, floated in a free-kick for West Ham team-mate Geoff Hurst to head the equaliser.** Martin Peters' close-range goal 12 minutes from time looked to have won the World Cup for Ramsey's England, but West Germany made it 2-2 in the dying seconds.

It was a match of almost unbearable tension and there was still more to come. Hurst's shot from Alan Ball's cross in extra-time hit the underside of the bar and bounced down inches over the line, according to the Russian linesman. Moore, still calm and collected, lofted a long pass upfield for Hurst to blast home a fourth goal for England. He remains the only player to have scored a hat-trick in a World Cup Final.

Four years later the teams met again in a World Cup quarter final in Mexico '70 and things began to go wrong for England before the match had even started. Gordon Banks, the brilliant goalkeeper, went down with a stomach bug and had to be replaced. England were still 2-0 up by the 49th minute and apparently coasting to victory, but the match ended in a shock 3-2 defeat.

There were epic duels with West Germany in a World Cup Semi-Final in 1990 and with Germany in a European Championship Semi-Final six years later, both of which the Germans won on penalties. But **there was a night of pure joy for England fans as Germany were humbled 5-1 in Munich in a critical World Cup qualifier in 2001**. Michael Owen scored a hat-trick – the first by an England player against a German team since Geoff Hurst – and Steven Gerrard and Emile Heskey weighed in with the others. It was Svensational!

RIVAL

European Qualifying Group 9
Germany v England
Olympic Stadium - Munich
01.09.2001

BOBBY CHARLTON

MIDFIELDER   1958-70   106 CAPS   49 GOALS

Charlton played for United more than anyone else (**606 appearances**) and scored a number of goals at that time (199).

Having **survived the Munich Air Crash**, Charlton helped inspired Manchester United to the European Cup and England to the World Cup. Once he received his England call-up, his reputation as a skilful midfielder with a **trademark long-range shot** grew rapidly. He scored hat-tricks against the USA in 1959 and Mexico two years later.

Charlton sits at the top of the England goal scoring charts with 49. By the time he scored against Argentina in the 1962 World Cup Finals, he had found the net 25 times in 38 appearances.

WORLD CUP FINAL ENGLAND V WEST GERMANY ENGLAND'S BOBBY CHARLTON CELEBRATES THE CONTROVERSIAL THIRD GOAL 30.07.1966

ENGLAND

For the 1966 World Cup, Alf Ramsey built the team around Bobby Charlton. One of the most famous goals in Three Lions history was the opener of a match against Mexico, where he took a 25-yard shot into the top corner of the Mexico net. In the Final, both Charltons played key roles in the victory over West Germany.

ALAN BALL

HOME INTERNATIONAL CHAMPIONSHIP
SCOTLAND V ENGLAND
HAMPDEN PARK
02.04.1966

Ball was rejected many times by various clubs, told that he was too small (5ft 6in) to be a footballer. Eventually he secured a place at Blackpool by the age of 17.

His combination of **aggressive tackling**, **tireless running** and a **strong desire to win** brought him recognition. He wanted to be on the international stage and he finally reached it at just 3 days short of his 20th birthday.

LEGENDS

MIDFIELDER   1965-75   72 CAPS   8 GOALS

Full of energy, Alan Ball was drafted into Alf Ramsey's England squad for the 1966 World Cup. He was the **youngest member of the cup-winning team**. The Final was the midfielder's finest 120 minutes in an England shirt – he expended so much energy on the pitch that he felt he had 'already died twice' by the end.

DAVID BECKHAM

David Beckham joined the list of England greats when he won his **100th international cap** against France in March 2008, becoming only the fifth player in history to reach this milestone. In February 2009, Beckham equalled Bobby Moore's record as the two most capped outfield players for England – sharing the title on 108 caps.

BORN 02.05.75, Leytonstone
POSITION Midfielder
CLUB AC Milan (on loan)
CAPS 110
ENGLAND DEBUT 01.09.96, against Moldova

International Friendly
Spain v England
Ramon Sanchez-Pizjuan Stadium - Seville
11.02.2009

PLAYER

STEVEN GERRARD

Steven Gerrard's **speed**, **strength** and **skill** on the ball make him one of the most talented midfielders around. The Liverpool captain was awarded the 2007 **Nationwide England Player of the Year** trophy two days before the Three Lions took on Switzerland in early 2008. By the end of 2008, Gerrard had taken his goal tally to an impressive 14 strikes in 70 games.

BORN 30.05.80, Liverpool
POSITION Midfielder
CLUB Liverpool
CAPS 72
ENGLAND DEBUT 31.05.00, against Ukraine

World Cup 2010
Qualifying Round Group 6
England v Ukraine
Wembley Stadium - London
01.04.2009

JOLEON LESCOTT

As a result of his impressive play for Everton, Lescott was called up into the senior squad for the first time for the Euro 2008 qualifiers with Israel and Russia. The Everton defender was named in a number of Fabio Capello's squads during 2008 and made his first outing under Capello against France that year.

BORN 16.08.82, Birmingham
POSITION Centre-back
CLUB Everton
CAPS 6
ENGLAND DEBUT 13.10.07, against Estonia

World Cup 2010
Qualifying Round Group 6
Andorra v England
Olympic Stadium - Barcelona
06.09.2008

PROFILES

JERMAIN DEFOE

International Friendly
Germany v England
Olympic Stadium
Berlin
19.11.2008

Defoe's strong form at club level, for both Portsmouth and Tottenham Hotspur, has propelled him into the international **spotlight**. He has become a regular in the England team, doubling his international goal tally in 2008. Defoe played his part in the good start that has been made to the World Cup qualifying campaign.

BORN 07.10.82, Beckton
POSITION Striker
CLUB Tottenham Hotspur
CAPS 32
ENGLAND DEBUT 31.03.04, against Sweden

QUIZ

What year did England win the World Cup?

1962 1966 1970

Who wasn't an England Manager?

Alf Ramsey Bobby Robson Martin O'Neill

What position does Gareth Barry play in for England?

Striker Defender Midfielder

Since 1950, how many times have England failed to qualify for the World Cup?

2 3 4

Who was the last team to win the European Championship?

Spain Italy France

Which player won the Golden Boot award at the 1986 World Cup?

Bryan Robson Gary Lineker Alan Shearer

1-3 answers correct

Nice try! It's time to hit the books and swat up on your footballing knowledge.

4-5 answers correct

Not bad, but you could do better. Don't just read the headlines, get stuck in and find out about the history of the great game.

6 answers correct

Perfect! You certainly know your football. Keep up the good work.

Answers: 1966, Martin O'Neill, Midfielder, 3, Spain and Gary Lineker.

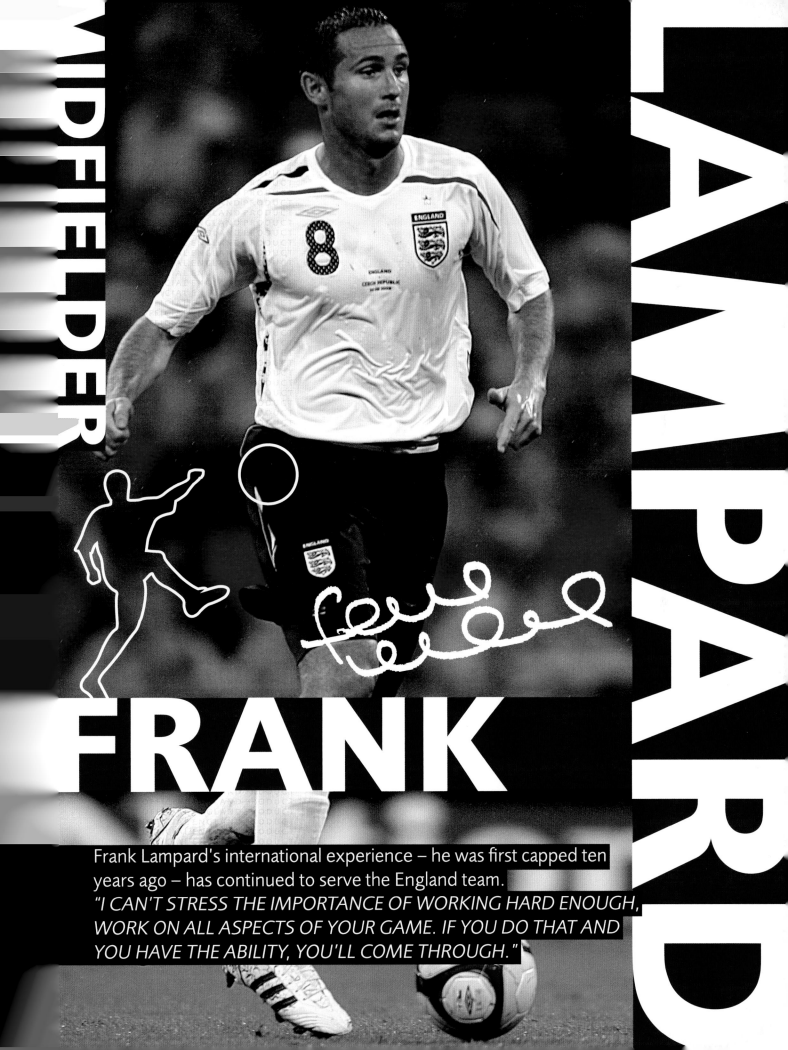

MIDFIELDER

LAMPARD

FRANK

Frank Lampard's international experience – he was first capped ten years ago – has continued to serve the England team.

"I CAN'T STRESS THE IMPORTANCE OF WORKING HARD ENOUGH, WORK ON ALL ASPECTS OF YOUR GAME. IF YOU DO THAT AND YOU HAVE THE ABILITY, YOU'LL COME THROUGH."

STRIKER

CROUCH

PETER

Crouch was confident that once he was a valuable member of a top league team his chance to play for England would come, and it did!

"I'VE GOT MY OWN TARGETS, ...
TO ESTABLISH MYSELF IN THE TEAM AND ONCE YOU ARE A REGULAR FOR YOUR TEAM THEN ENGLAND [RECOGNITION] COMES FROM THAT AND HOPEFULLY THIS WILL PROVE THE CASE."

PLAYER LINE UP

NAME THE PLAYER LINE UP

WORLD CUP 2010
QUALIFYING ROUND
GROUP 6
BELARUS V ENGLAND
DINAMO STADIUM - MINSK
15.10.2008

Answers: England's (left to right, bottom row) Wes Brown, Steven Gerrard, Wayne Bridge, Wayne Rooney, Theo Walcott, (top row) Emile Heskey, Rio Ferdinand, David James, Matthew Upson, Gareth Barry and Frank Lampard.

FABIO CAPELLO

Fabio Capello was appointed England Manager on Friday 14 December 2007.

His **16-year managerial career** has encompassed spells at AC Milan, Real Madrid, AS Roma and Juventus. In total, Capello has won nine League titles in Italy and Spain as well as lifting the European Cup with Milan in 1994.

Capello enjoyed a successful playing career as a midfielder with Roma, Juventus and Milan, winning 32 caps for Italy. He began his coaching career with Milan graduating to take charge of the first team in 1991. He brought huge success to the club winning four Serie A titles in five seasons and overseeing European Cup success with a 4-0 Final victory over Barcelona in 1994.

A season at Real Madrid followed where the team won La Liga. After a brief return to Milan, Capello joined Roma. The Serie A title was secured in 2001 and Capello was recruited by Juventus in 2004 where he won Serie A in both 2005 and 2006. Capello spent the next season back at Real Madrid, once again winning the League.

DATE OF BIRTH June 18, 1946
PLACE OF BIRTH Gorizia, Italy
MANAGED 13
WON 9
LOST 2
DRAWS 1
GOALS 31
GOALS CONCEDED 11

POLAND

There was a time when England always seemed to be drawn against Poland in the qualifying groups for major tournaments. In a ten-year period the two teams met in three World Cups and two European Championships. But there were two hugely significant fixtures before that – in 1973 and 1986.

England had been hosts and holders for the two World Cups before the one staged by West Germany in 1974. Now obliged to qualify, the team had already lost 2-0 in Poland and went into the return knowing that only a victory would take them through to the Finals.

THERE WAS A TIME WHEN ENGLAND ALWAYS SEEMED TO BE DRAWN AGAINST POLAND IN THE QUALIFYING GROUPS FOR MAJOR TOURNAMENTS

GREAT

World Cup Mexico
England v Poland
Gary Lineker scores for England
11.06.1986

With 100,000 people packed into Wembley, England immediately tore into the opposition. But **Polish goalkeeper Tomaszewski had an inspired night, blocking shots and headers with every part of his body**. After an hour of incessant England pressure, the unthinkable happened and Domarski squeezed a shot under Shilton.

Allan Clarke thumped home an equaliser from the penalty mark six minutes later, but Poland survived a further onslaught to claim the 1-1 draw that clinched their own qualification. One national newspaper carried the headline *"It's the end of the world!"*.

It was all or nothing for England in their last group match with the Poles in the 1986 World Cup in Mexico. The pressure on Bobby Robson's team was intense, as defeat would send them home. But by the **26th minute Gary Lineker had scored a fabulous hat-trick and England's pride was restored with a 3-0 victory**.

Lineker again had an important role to play when England played their final Euro '92 qualifier in Poznan. Initially it seemed that Poland were destined to grab the glory,

But Lineker, England's inspirational captain, volleyed a spectacular 77th-minute equaliser that took England through to the Swedish Finals.

Kevin Keegan, who had won 63 caps as a player, was a popular choice as England manager and importantly he started with a win. His team beat Poland 3-1 in the Wembley sunshine in a Euro 2000 qualifier. **Paul Scholes, the Manchester United midfielder, scored a splendid hat-trick.**

David Beckham celebrates with team-mate Paul Scholes after Scholes scored the second of his three goals against Poland during their Euro 2000 qualifying match at Wembley. 27.03.1999

Fabio Capello believes that England's team spirit has been the most important improvement during his first year in charge.

The Three Lions Manager, who was appointed on 14 December 2007, gave his end-of-year assessment at The FA's headquarters in Soho Square.

And, after eight victories, one draw and one defeat in his first ten games in charge, he could be pleased with the way things have gone.

England topped 2010 FIFA World Cup Qualifying Group Six, after impressive away wins over Croatia and Belarus.

INTERNATIONAL FRIENDLY
SPAIN V ENGLAND
FABIO CAPELLO
ENGLAND MANAGER
11.02.2009

But **Capello believes that the team improved their attitude and belief** after losing 1-0 to France in March 2008, and this in turn has bred confidence - and match-winning performances.

He said: *"I am happy for the result and I am happy with what we did to create a group mentality and team spirit. We have managed to recover the confidence [of the players] - this was the most important work that we did."*

"The spirit of the squad has been great, and most important. Without that spirit in the group, the confidence will not be there and it is impossible to win. Sometimes you can win one game because one player has scored a goal. But without the spirit it is impossible."

Capello views his side's 1-0 defeat to France in his second game in charge as the turning point in England's fortunes - simply because he **made them believe**.

"I knew before we played France it would be hard, as they have been world champions. And we played in France, and in Paris. For half-an-hour we played very well. And when you can play well for half-an-hour, you can play well for the whole game. After this game, because of that reason, we moved forward."

"The door of the national team is always open. I will check before the next international game. I will then decide if he is ready, if he is OK. The most important thing will be if he is fit."

REVIEW

"I realised that the problem was in the mind of the players. Now we are better. We need time and we will continue to work. It is important to be a psychologist but we need good players to win. Good psychologist, bad players - it is impossible to win. We want to be better."

Michael Owen, the Newcastle United striker and captain, could be involved in a future England squad too, says Capello - despite only featuring in the second half versus France in 2008.

Capello also praised Aston Villa's young forwards Ashley Young and Gabriel Agbonlahor, and tipped them to star for England in the near future.

He added: *"I am very happy for the players who play at Aston Villa. I also like [James] Milner, who is another young player. These players are the future, and it is a bright future."*

JAMES MILNER

BORN 04.01.86, Leeds
POSITION Midfielder
CLUB Aston Villa
CAPS 0

After a long spell in the Under-21s, in which Milner was the **top scorer** in 2008, the Aston Villa midfielder had his first call up to the Senior squad in a friendly against Spain in February 2009. He never came on as a sub, but his impressive form will be sure to secure another place in the squad in the near future.

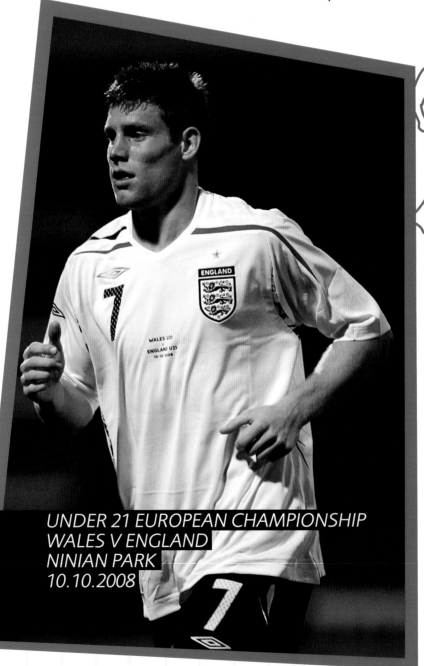

UNDER 21 EUROPEAN CHAMPIONSHIP
WALES V ENGLAND
NINIAN PARK
10.10.2008

"WITH THE PLAYERS WE HAVE HAD IN THE [UNDER-21S] SQUAD SINCE I'VE BEEN INVOLVED, AND EVEN BEFORE, ENGLAND HAVE HAD SOME VERY TALENTED PLAYERS, BUT WE HAVEN'T WON THE EUROPEAN CHAMPIONSHIP FOR A LONG TIME."

BORN 13.10.86, Erdington
POSITION Forward
CLUB Aston Villa
CAPS 2

Gabriel made his first senior team outing in a friendly against Germany in November 2008. The Aston Villa striker had a **good debut**, challenging the German defence on several occasions in the first half. Agbonlahor is eligible to play international football for Nigeria and Scotland, but he wants to succeed in securing a spot in the England squad.

INTERNATIONAL FRIENDLY
GERMANY V ENGLAND
OLYMPIC STADIUM BERLIN
19.11.2008

GABRIEL AGBONLAHOR

"IF I DIDN'T GET THE CHANCE FOR ENGLAND, THEN HE [MY DAD] WOULD HAVE WANTED ME PLAYING FOR NIGERIA, BUT ENGLAND IS NUMBER ONE."

51

BRYAN ROBSON

MIDFIELDER   1980-91   90 CAPS   26 GOALS

*INTERNATIONAL WORLD CUP WARM-UP
TUNISIA V ENGLAND
02.06.1990*

Bryan Robson, known as **Captain Marvel**, was the most complete midfielder of his day and one of the **finest players to wear an England shirt** in the 1980s and 90s.

The Manchester United man was an important part of Bobby Robson's England squad that qualified for the World Cup Finals for the first time since 1970. In the first game against France, he scored one of the **fastest goals in the history** of the Finals.

Robson would have reached the 100 cap mark for his country if it wasn't for injury, which caused him to miss games in the 1986 and 1990 World Cups. His best goal was probably a **spectacular volley against East Germany** in a friendly in 1984.

ENGLAND

"HE WAS THREE PLAYERS IN ONE – A TACKLER, A GOAL MAKER AND A GOAL TAKER."
Sir Bobby Robson

GARY LINEKER

STRIKER 1984-92 80 CAPS 48 GOALS

*INTERNATIONAL FRIENDLY
ENGLAND V HUNGARY
12.09.1990*

Gary Lineker is one of the **greatest forwards** that English football has ever produced. He scored 48 international goals in 80 matches for his country, leaving him only one short of Sir Bobby Charlton's England record.

Lineker's scoring abilities made him the only English **winner of the World Cup Golden Boot**, a result of his six goals in the 1986 tournament in Mexico.

Lineker retained his form at the 1990 World Cup in Italy, making four vital strikes en route to the Semi-Finals.

He played his last game for England against Sweden in Euro 92, eight years after he had made his international debut against Scotland.

LEGENDS

Famously, Lineker was never sent off nor received a yellow card throughout a playing career that started in his hometown club Leicester, in 1976. He scored nearly 100 goals in just under 200 games for his club.

"I KNEW I COULD SCORE GOALS. MY GAME WAS ALL ABOUT GAMBLING, FINDING SPACE. A LITTLE BIT LIKE MICHAEL OWEN, ONCE I'D PLAYED IN A FEW GAMES AND SCORED, I COULD KEEP MY CALM AND KNOCK THEM IN."

FRANK LAMPARD

BORN 20.06.78, Romford
POSITION Midfielder
CLUB Chelsea
CAPS 69
ENGLAND DEBUT 10.10.99, against Belgium

*International Friendly
Germany v England
Olympic Stadium
19.11.2008*

Awarded the **Official Player of the Year** in both 2004 and 2005, Lampard is one of the most popular and **talented** England players. He was an ever-present in the second half of 2008, starting five out of six matches. Lampard helped to create the second goal of Theo Walcott's hat-trick in Croatia and he set up the first two goals in the 5-1 win against Kazakhstan in the 2010 World Cup qualifiers.

PLAYER

Wright-Phillips is one of the few current England stars to have **scored on his international debut** after scoring his first goal against the Ukraine in 2004. As one of England's most **dangerous attacking** players, he made four victorious England appearances in 2008 and scored the winning goal in Fabio Capello's first match in charge.

*International Friendly
Germany v England
Olympic Stadium
Berlin
19.11.2008*

BORN 25.10.81, Greenwich
POSITION Midfielder
CLUB Manchester City
CAPS 24
ENGLAND DEBUT 18.08.04, against Ukraine

SHAUN WRIGHT-PHILLIPS

PETER CROUCH

BORN 30.01.81, Macclesfield
POSITION Striker
CLUB Portsmouth
CAPS 33
ENGLAND DEBUT 31.05.05, against Colombia

Scoring 17 goals in the 2004-05 season for previous club side Southampton, Peter Crouch earned a call-up for the USA Tour in May 2005. In 2008, Crouch switched clubs from Liverpool to FA Cup winners Portsmouth, and all of his caps under Fabio Capello came from the bench. Despite not scoring in his six 2008 appearances, Crouch is still close to a goal every two games for England.

World Cup 2010
Qualifying Round Group 6
England v Ukraine
Wembley Stadium - London
01.04.2009

PROFILES

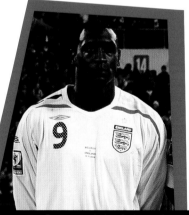

World Cup 2010
Qualifying Round Group 6
Belarus v England
Dinamo Stadium - Minsk
15.10.2008

BORN 11.01.78, Leicester
POSITION Striker
CLUB Aston Villa
CAPS 52
ENGLAND DEBUT 28.04.99, against Hungary

Powerful, quick and physically imposing, Heskey is a **bulldozer** of a centre-forward. He made his first international appearance under Fabio Capello in the Czech Republic friendly in August 2008. He had such an impact in that match that Capello called on him on four other occasions that year, all in World Cup qualifiers. He has continuously displayed an **impressive form** throughout England's qualifying campaign.

EMILE HESKEY

MATCH MOMENTS

DRAW A CIRCLE AROUND THE YEAR THAT THE GAME TOOK PLACE.

1950

1966

1996

2000

Answers: 1966 – England's Geoff Hurst heads the equalising goal in the 1966 World Cup Final. 1996 – Paul Gascoigne celebrates his goal with Teddy Sheringham in the Euro 96 clash against Scotland.

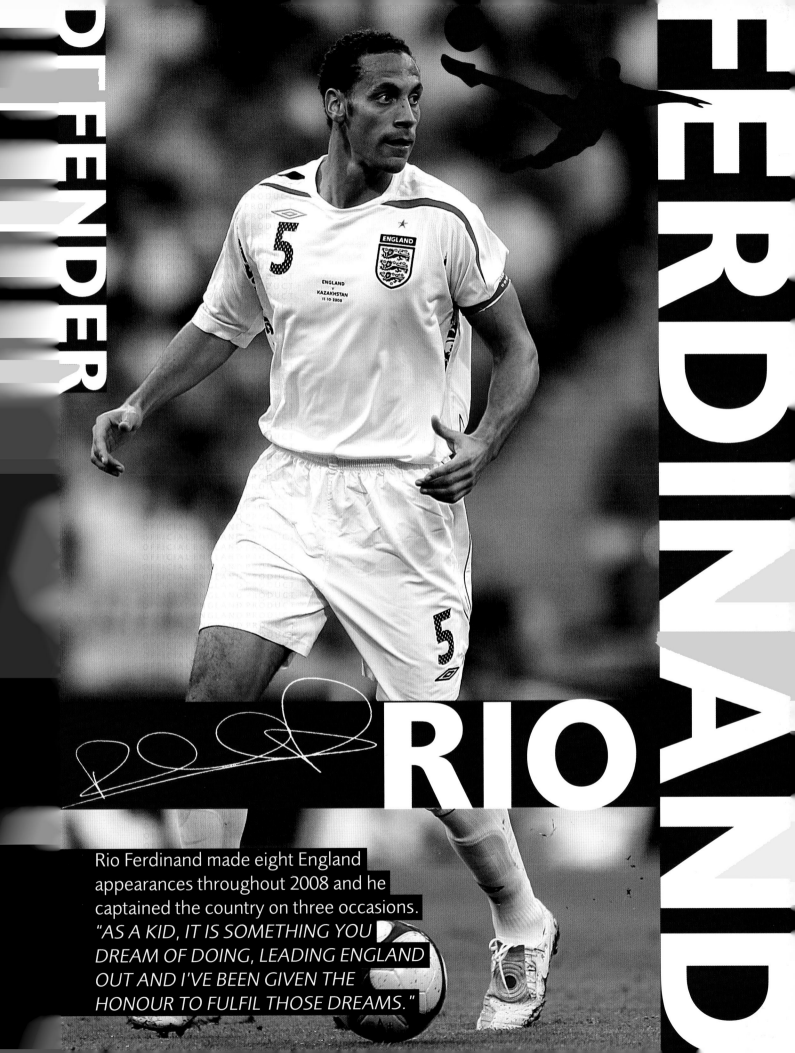

DEFENDER

RIO FERDINAND

RIO

Rio Ferdinand made eight England appearances throughout 2008 and he captained the country on three occasions. *"AS A KID, IT IS SOMETHING YOU DREAM OF DOING, LEADING ENGLAND OUT AND I'VE BEEN GIVEN THE HONOUR TO FULFIL THOSE DREAMS."*

GARETH BARRY

MIDFIELDER

Gareth Barry is yet to miss a game under Fabio Capello and he was the only outfield player to play in every game of 2008.

"IT GIVES YOU THAT CONFIDENCE BEFORE YOU MEET UP WITH THE SQUAD, KNOWING YOU'VE BEEN INVOLVED FOR NEAR ON TWO YEARS AND PLAYED IN VIRTUALLY EVERY GAME. IT'S GOOD FOR MYSELF TO BE INVOLVED LIKE THAT AND IT DOES HELP WHEN YOU COME TO PLAY THE GAMES, KNOWING THE OTHER PLAYERS' GAMES AND THE MANAGER'S IDEAS AS WELL."

WORLD CUP 2010
QUALIFYING ROUND GROUP 6
ANDORRA V ENGLAND
OLYMPIC STADIUM - BARCELONA
06.09.2008

SPOT THE

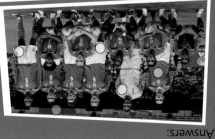

DIFFERENCES

BRAZIL

Brazil, five times World Cup winners, have always proved difficult opponents for England. The Three Lions have only won three of the 22 matches played, but did win the first encounter played at Wembley in 1956. A capacity 100,000 crowd saw penalty misses by England's John Atyeo and Roger Byrne, but the home side still won impressively 4-2.

be remembered for a goalkeeper's save. Jairzinho outpaced Terry Cooper down the right and lofted in a cross that the great Pelé met with a powerful downward header seven yards out. But Gordon Banks flew across his goal and somehow managed to flick the ball up and over the bar with his right hand.

England v Brazil
Wembley - London
England's Gary Lineker (l) celebrates after scoring the only goal of the game with Terry Butcher. David Platt runs in (r).
28.03.1990

GREAT

Then England met the Brazilians in three World Cup tournaments out of four. **There was a 0-0 draw in Sweden in 1958, the first goalless match in Finals history**, and Brazil inspired by Garrincha won 3-1 in a Quarter-final on their way to retaining the Jules Rimet Trophy in Chile four years later. England, then the holders, took on the unstoppable Brazilians in Mexico in 1970 and lost a group match 1-0 that will always

Against all the odds in 1984, **England became the first visiting team to beat Brazil at Maracana Stadium for 27 years**. Moments before half-time John Barnes left a trail of defenders behind him before calmly placing the ball beyond Roberto Costa's reach. Mark Hateley's far-post header from Barnes' cross made it 2-0 for England's first win against Brazil in 12 attempts.

An all-seater Wembley was filled to its 80,000 capacity for the first time when England last defeated the charismatic Brazilians in 1990. **Gary Lineker scored from Peter Beardsley's near-post corner for the only goal. England had now remained unbeaten for 15 matches since the Euro '88 Finals**.

Brazil looked to be 'awesome in attack' and 'vulnerable in defence' when England met them in a World Cup Quarter-final in Shizuoka in 2002. Michael Owen took advantage of Lucio's mistake to calmly chip Sven's England in front, but crucially Brazil levelled moments before half-time. Then Ronaldinho's freakish free-kick deceived David Seaman to make it 2-1. England were unable to equalise in the intense head and lost the match.

BRAZIL, THE FIVE TIMES WORLD CUP WINNERS, HAVE ALWAYS PROVED TO BE DIFFICULT OPPONENTS FOR ENGLAND

RIVAL

*World Cup - Quarter-final
England v Brazil
England's Emile Heskey (r) shrugs off
the challenge of Brazil's Roque Junior
21.06.2002*

ALAN SHEARER

EURO 2000 QUALIFIER - GROUP 5
LUXEMBOURG V ENGLAND
14.10.1998

Alan Shearer was known as the **perfect centre-forward**, a strong player who possessed the **hardest shot** since Bobby Charlton.

Shearer was destined for **stardom** in the world of football from the day he made his full debut, scoring a **hat-trick** for Southampton in a 4-2 victory over Arsenal. He was the **first player to score 200 Premiership goals**.

STRIKER   1992-2000   63 CAPS   30 GOALS

ENGLAND

Shearer's finest moment was undoubtedly Euro' 96. He displayed his **true form** throughout the tournament, **winning the Golden Boot** as leading scorer.

Once Shearer was given the **captain's armband**, he went on to lead England 34 times.

TEDDY SHERINGHAM

WORLD CUP 2002 - GROUP F
NIGERIA V ENGLAND
12.06.2002

Teddy Sheringham is the **fifth-highest scorer in Premiership** history and has achieved nearly everything in the game including scoring in a Champions League Final for Manchester United and starring at Euro 1996.

A **superb finisher** in his own right, Sheringham was the perfect foil for Alan Shearer in England's impressive Euro 1996 side, and his **subtle skills** and **intelligent link-up play** were crucial to England's success. Their partnership at international level became known as 'The SAS' ('Shearer And Sheringham'). Their most famous contribution was in the 4-1 victory over Holland, where they both scored twice.

STRIKER   1993-02   51 CAPS   11 GOALS

LEGENDS

Sheringham was selected as part of Eriksson's 2002 World Cup squad and played in the famous 1-0 win against Argentina. He made his final England appearance at the age of 36.

CROSS

1. How many groups are there in the group stages of the 2010 World Cup? (5)
3. This player was awarded the official player of the year in both 2004 and 2005. (5,7)
6. England scored 13 goals against this team in one game on two separate occasions. (7)
7. The colour of the England away kit. (3)
8. This team won the 2006 World Cup. (5)
9. England goalkeeper, _____ James. (5)
10. The current England Manager. (5,7)
11. This player matched Bobby Moore's 108 Caps for England record in February 2009. (5,7)
13. The country England played their first ever international against in 1872. (8)
15. David Beckham has a film named after him. _____ it like Beckham. (4)
18. Name the team that is missing in England's World Cup qualifying group. Belarus, Croatia, Kazakhstan, Ukraine. (7)
19. The most capped England player, with 125 caps. (5,7)
20. This player scored the most goals for England, an incredible 49. (5,8)

2. How many lions feature on the England Crest? (5)
4. Stewart Downing's position. (10)
5. The 2010 World Cup will be held in… (5,6)
12. This former England player was the first to score 200 Premiership goals. (4,7)
14. Name the youngest ever player to play for England. (4,7)
16. Ashley Cole plays in this position. (7)
17. The current England captain. (4,5)

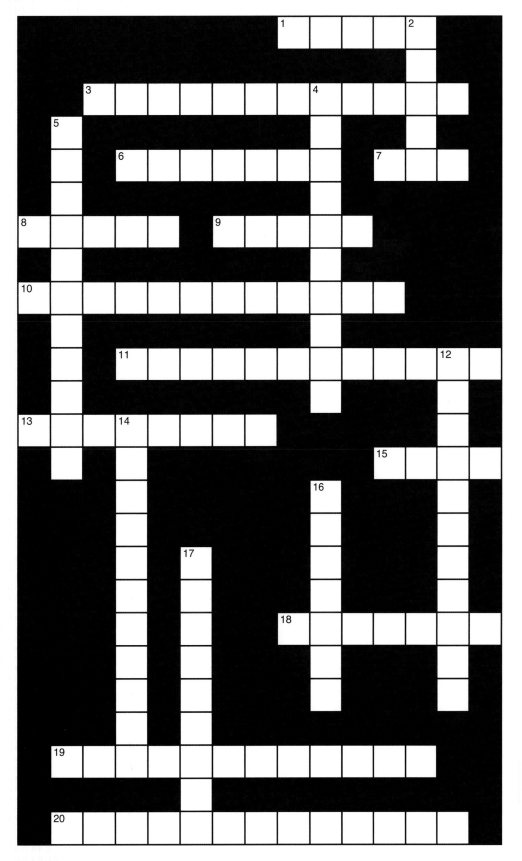

Answers:

From glorious campaigns that united the whole country, like Euro 1996, Italia 1990 and, of course, the **1966 World Cup win**, to the disappointing displays

ENGLAND, WORLD CUP WINNERS, 1966

and feelings of injustice that have left a bitter taste in the mouth, such as the Euro 2004 exit and **Maradona's infamous 'hand of God'**, England have played their part in some of football's most memorable moments.

The **hosts of the World Cup have also been the eventual winners on six occasions**, including England's 1966 success.

As **three-time winners, Uruguay, Italy and Brazil** would have been presented with the **Jules Rimet trophy** to keep, had they won the World Cup in 1966.

Brazil did manage to get their hands on the trophy four years later, after claiming the 1970 title.

Before the 1966 World Cup in England, the **Jules Rimet trophy was stolen from an exhibition**. Thankfully it was later recovered by a dog named Pickles.

Two players scored for England at the 1950 Finals, **Wilf Mannion**, the Middlesbrough striker, and **Stan Mortensen**, the Blackpool centre-forward.

THE HOSTS OF THE WORLD CUP HAVE ALSO BEEN THE EVENTUAL WINNERS ON SIX OCCASIONS.

THE TWO

ENGLAND AND WEST GERMANY LINE-UP FOR THE 1966 WORLD CUP FINAL AT WEMBLEY.

WORLD CUP PERFORMANCES

YEAR	HOSTS	ENGLAND'S PERFORMANCE	WINNERS
1930	Uruguay	Did not enter	Uruguay
1934	Italy	Did not enter	Italy
1938	France	Did not enter	Italy
1950	Brazil	Round 1	Uruguay
1954	Switzerland	Quarter-finals	West Germany
1958	Sweden	Round 1	Brazil
1962	Chile	Quarter-finals	Brazil
1966	**England**	**Winners**	**England**
1970	Mexico	Quarter-finals	Brazil
1974	West Germany	Did not qualify	West Germany
1978	Argentina	Did not qualify	Argentina
1982	Spain	Round 2	Italy
1986	Mexico	Quarter-finals	Argentina
1990	Italy	Semi-finals	West Germany
1994	USA	Did not qualify	Brazil
1998	France	Round 2	France
2002	Japan & South Korea	Quarter-finals	Brazil
2006	Germany	Quarter-finals	Italy

RLD CUP

BOBBY MOORE, MARTIN PETERS & GEOFF HURST CELEBRATING AT WEMBLEY IN 1966.

Alf Ramsey's England team memorably won the World Cup in 1966, when West Germany were defeated 4-2 after extra-time at the old Wembley. **England also reached the Semi-finals in 1990 and made the Quarter-finals on no fewer than six occasions**.

When The FA rejoined FIFA after the war, England finally became eligible to take part in the World Cup. However, after losing to the American team of part-timers in Brazil in 1950, England were on their way home after the First Round.

England then failed to qualify for the tournaments of 1974 and 1978. Ron Greenwood took England to the Finals in Spain in 1982, where although unbeaten, they went out in the Second Round. **Things looked more promising in Mexico in 1986, until Maradona scored both goals as Argentina beat England 2-1 in the Quarter-finals**.

THE WO

Bobby Charlton played a crucial role in England's re-emergence in the 1960s, alongside team-mates Gordon Banks, Bobby Moore and Martin Peters. **England were World Cup winners on home soil and travelled to Mexico in 1970 with an even stronger squad, losing dramatically to West Germany in the Quarter-finals**.

Frustration dogged the next three tournaments - **England came within a penalty shootout of reaching the Final in 1990**, failed to qualify in 1994, and were **knocked out by Argentina in the Second Round of France '98, again on penalties**. Around 24 million people watched on the BBC as England gained revenge on their old rivals four years later, winning 1-0.

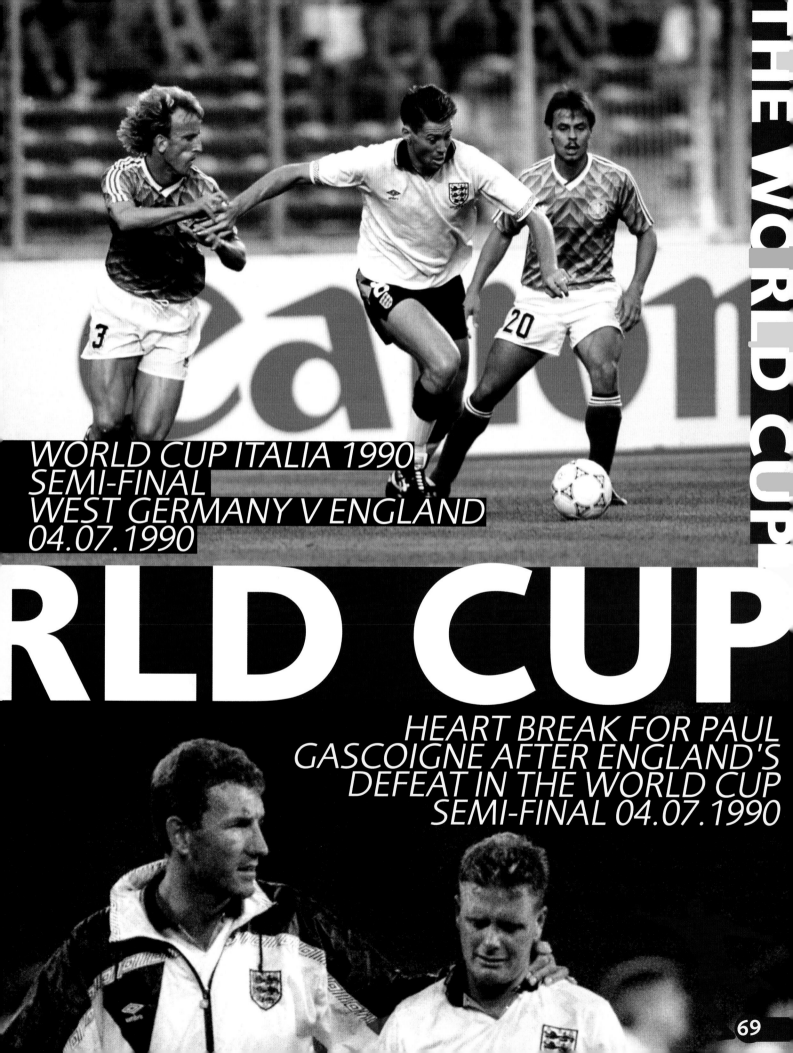

WORLD CUP ITALIA 1990
SEMI-FINAL
WEST GERMANY V ENGLAND
04.07.1990

RLD CUP

HEART BREAK FOR PAUL
GASCOIGNE AFTER ENGLAND'S
DEFEAT IN THE WORLD CUP
SEMI-FINAL 04.07.1990

JOE COLE

BORN 08.11.81, Islington
POSITION Midfielder
CLUB Chelsea
CAPS 53
ENGLAND DEBUT 25.05.01, against Mexico

Joe Cole uses his **superb skill** to beat defenders and dribble the ball at a **fast pace**. He has been a regular on the England team since his 2001 debut and his **long-range volley** against Sweden in the 2006 World Cup was one of the best goals in the tournament. Cole started 2008 by setting up the first goal under Fabio Capello and grabbed his first goal of that year in August.

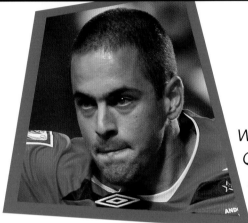

World Cup 2010
Qualifying Round Group 6
Andorra v England
Olympic Stadium - Barcelona
06.09.2008

PLAYER P

Jermaine Jenas was **voted the 2002/03 PFA Young Player of the Year** and is developing into one of the **best all-round midfielders** for England. In 2008, he was the Three Lions' first goalscorer of the year, when England faced Switzerland at Wembley.

International Friendly
England v Switzerland
Wembley Stadium - London
06.02.2008

BORN 18.02.83, Nottingham
POSITION Midfielder
CLUB Tottenham Hotspur
CAPS 20
ENGLAND DEBUT 12.02.03, against Australia

JERMAINE JENAS

WAYNE ROONEY

BORN 24.10.85, Liverpool
POSITION Striker
CLUB Manchester United
CAPS 50
ENGLAND DEBUT 12.02.03, against Australia

Wayne Rooney is still one of the most **exciting** and **talented** players England has ever produced. 2008 proved a very successful year for Rooney; not only did he help Manchester United to the Premier and Champions League titles, he also played a major role in helping England top their World Cup qualifying group.

World Cup 2010
Qualifying Round Group 6
England v Ukraine
Wembley Stadium - London
01.04.2009

PROFILES

World Cup 2010
Qualifying Round Group 6
Belarus v England
Dinamo Stadium - Minsk
15.10.2008

Theo Walcott became England's **youngest ever player** aged just 17 years and 75 days when he made his debut in 2006. Coming on for Michael Owen in his first senior match, Walcott beat Rooney's previous record as England's youngest cap. Walcott was part of Capello's starting eleven for the 2010 World Cup qualifier away to Croatia. It was here he became the youngest ever player to **score a hat-trick**.

BORN 16.03.89, London
POSITION Striker
CLUB Arsenal
CAPS 6
ENGLAND DEBUT 30.05.06, against Hungary

THEO WALCOTT

WORDSEARCH

CHARLTON, Bobby 49
LINEKER, Gary 48
GREAVES, Jimmy 44
OWEN, Michael 40
FINNEY, Tom 30
LOFTHOUSE, Nat 30
SHEARER, Alan 30
WOODWARD, Vivian 29
BLOOMER, Stephen 28
PLATT, David 27

```
W D R N C H A R L T O N
Y Z O X O Z R E R R K F
L I Z N X E K D E H I I
K X K A M C R R D L L N
H C P O T A A Q A O I N
F I O H W E O R F F N E
F L N D H T T E V T E Y
B A O S O T O A J H K N
F O Z G A R U B T O E I
W W K L N N X P E U R E
V E P G R E A V E S B D
H N J U Y S O X N E Q M
```

FIND ENGLAND'S TOP 10 SCORERS OF ALL TIME IN THIS GRID

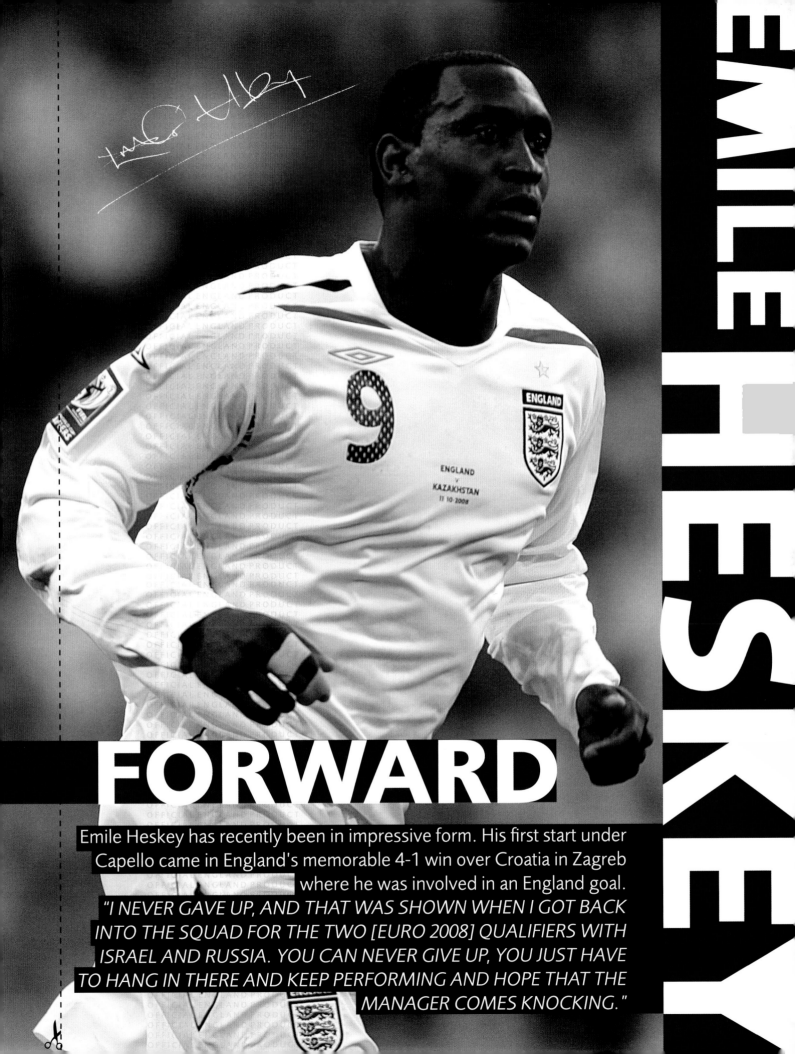

FORWARD

Emile Heskey has recently been in impressive form. His first start under Capello came in England's memorable 4-1 win over Croatia in Zagreb where he was involved in an England goal.

"I NEVER GAVE UP, AND THAT WAS SHOWN WHEN I GOT BACK INTO THE SQUAD FOR THE TWO [EURO 2008] QUALIFIERS WITH ISRAEL AND RUSSIA. YOU CAN NEVER GIVE UP, YOU JUST HAVE TO HANG IN THERE AND KEEP PERFORMING AND HOPE THAT THE MANAGER COMES KNOCKING."

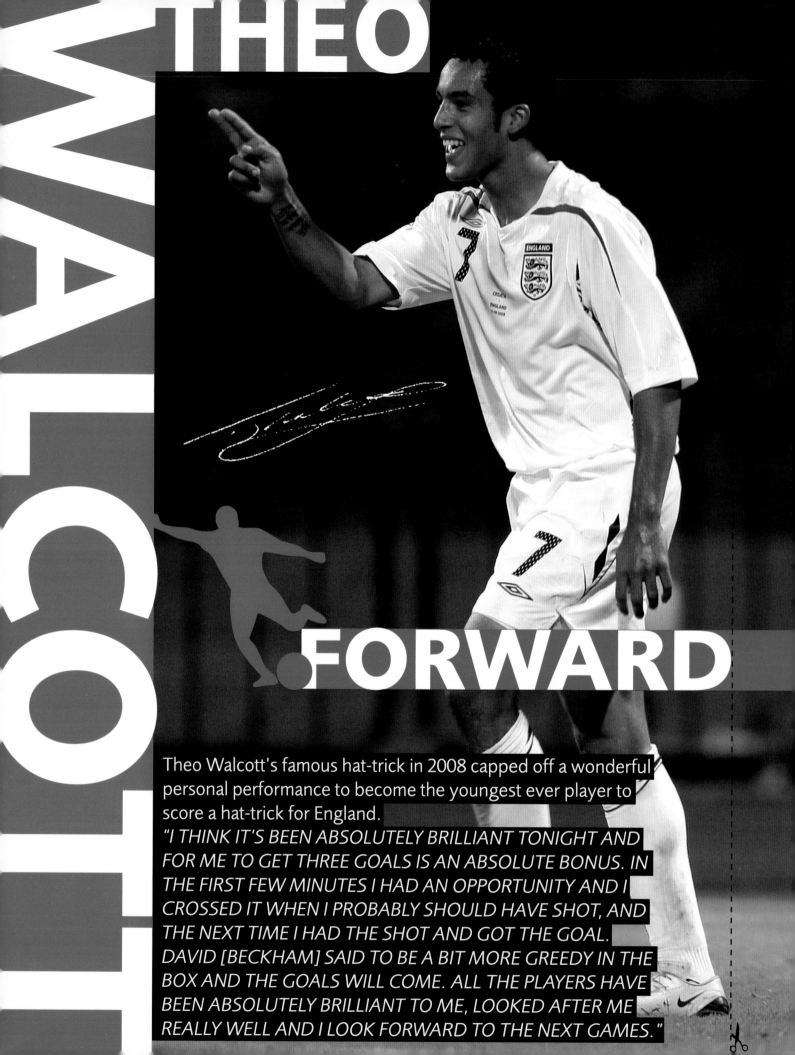

THEO WALCOTT

FORWARD

Theo Walcott's famous hat-trick in 2008 capped off a wonderful personal performance to become the youngest ever player to score a hat-trick for England.

"I THINK IT'S BEEN ABSOLUTELY BRILLIANT TONIGHT AND FOR ME TO GET THREE GOALS IS AN ABSOLUTE BONUS. IN THE FIRST FEW MINUTES I HAD AN OPPORTUNITY AND I CROSSED IT WHEN I PROBABLY SHOULD HAVE SHOT, AND THE NEXT TIME I HAD THE SHOT AND GOT THE GOAL. DAVID [BECKHAM] SAID TO BE A BIT MORE GREEDY IN THE BOX AND THE GOALS WILL COME. ALL THE PLAYERS HAVE BEEN ABSOLUTELY BRILLIANT TO ME, LOOKED AFTER ME REALLY WELL AND I LOOK FORWARD TO THE NEXT GAMES."

TRIVIA QUIZ

Who scored England's first goal of the 2006 World Cup?
Peter Crouch   Michael Carrick   Steven Gerrard

Who was the England manager for Euro 2004?
Steve McClaren   Sven-Goran Eriksson   Kevin Keegan

How often is the European Championship held?
Every two years   Every four years   Every six years

Who will be hosting Euro 2012?
Poland/Ukraine   Italy   Croatia/Hungary

Who were England playing against when Theo Walcott became their youngest ever hat-trick scorer?
Trinidad & Tobago   Switzerland   Croatia

What year was the last ever England game played at the old Wembley Stadium?
1999   2000   2001

A statue of which legendary England footballer stands outside the new Wembley Stadium?
Jimmy Greaves   Bobby Moore   Sir Geoff Hurst

Answers: Peter Crouch, Sven-Goran Eriksson, Every four years, Poland/Ukraine, Croatia, 2000, Bobby Moore.

DAVID PLATT

MIDFIELDER – 1989-96 – 62 CAPS – 27 GOALS

Platt's debut for the Three Lions came in November 1989 as they drew 0-0 with Italy at Wembley at 23 years old. The following year, a **memorable volley** created his first ever goal in an England shirt in the Italia 1990 World Cup.

Platt returned a hero from the 1990 World Cup and that season at Villa Park saw him score **19 League goals in 37 appearances** for the club. He moved to the Italian side Bari in 1991, which was the beginning of a four-year stint in Italy, also playing for clubs Juventus and Sampdoria.

INTERNATIONAL FRIENDLY
ENGLAND V HUNGARY
18.05.1996

ENGLAND

He was a member of the England squad for the 1996 European Championship, where he featured in four out of five games. England reached the semi-final but lost to Germany on penalties after a 1-1 draw in Platt's last match for his country.

Stuart Pearce played 78 times for England between 1987 and 1999 and for many he epitomised what wearing the Three Lions was all about. His **fast runs down the left**, solid free-kicks and **heart-on-sleeve** playing style won him cult status with England fans.

He made his international debut against Brazil in 1987 and was made England captain by Graham Taylor in 1991.

Pearce missed an all-important penalty shoot out shot against West Germany in the 1990 World Cup, but redeemed himself at Euro' 96. His **spot-kick** in a shoot out with Spain is one of England football's memorable moments.

INTERNATIONAL FRIENDLY
ENGLAND V ARGENTINA
25.05.1991

STUART PEARCE

DEFENDER 1987-99 78 CAPS 5 GOALS

LEGENDS

"I DIDN'T GIVE IN AND WAS PATIENT, AND THAT BROUGHT ITS OWN REWARDS. I WOULD HAVE TO SAY THAT TOURNAMENT WAS THE BEST TIME I HAVE EVER PLAYED FOOTBALL, AND THAT GAME AGAINST SPAIN STOOD OUT ON ITS OWN."

FAMOUS FIVE

Fabio Capello's England won five matches in a row, 2-0 v Andorra, 4-1 v Croatia, 5-1 v Kazakhstan, 3-1 v Belarus and 2-1 v Germany.

The last winning sequence as good as that, or better, happened between October 2005 and June 2006. Sven-Goran Eriksson's side won eight in a row before Sweden held them to a 2-2 draw during the World Cup Finals in Germany. **Five or more consecutive wins has now been achieved 17 times since the war** - by Capello, Eriksson (three times), Hoddle (once), Robson (twice), Greenwood (three times), Ramsey (four times) and Winterbottom (three times).

Eriksson's sides twice won eight in a row, the best figure post-war.

The best run ever, though, is ten in a row.

From June 1908 to June 1909 England won 6-1 and 11-1 v Austria, 7-0 v Hungary, 4-0 v Bohemia, 4-0 v Ireland, 2-0 v Wales, 2-0 v Scotland, 4-2 v Hungary, 8-2 v Hungary and 8-1 v Austria.

That was an average of 5.6 goals per match. Winterbottom's England were no slouches either - their results in six matches from October 1960 to May 1961 were 5-2, 9-0, 4-2, 5-1, 9-3 and 8-0. Jimmy Greaves contributed 11 goals, and Bobby Charlton and Bobby Smith eight each, as that England team managed an even better average of 6.6.
Capello's five, of course, included four away fixtures.

INTEREST

February 18 has been a particularly fruitful day in England's past. On that day in 1882 the England team achieved what is still their record score and record margin of victory, **humbling Ireland 13-0 in Belfast** in the first international between the two countries.

Aston Villa's Howard Vaughton scored the opening goal and finished with five. No player has managed more in a single England match. Villa team-mate Arthur Brown weighed in with four.

On the same day in 1899 England beat the Irish 13-2 at Roker Park. This is still England's biggest home win and 15 goals is still the record for an England fixture. Gilbert "GO" Smith was on target four times and Jimmy Crabtree took - and missed - England's first ever penalty.

Even in more modern times, February 18 has been a good day for England goals. In **1987 Bobby Robson's team won 4-2 against Spain in Madrid**, with Gary Lineker notching all four.

A DAY FOR GOALS

International football's oldest rivals are **England and Scotland**, who met in the first-ever match way back in 1872. **England and Scotland have now clashed 110 times on the football field**, with England having achieved 45 victories to Scotland's 41.

The Queen was present as Walter Winterbottom's England team thrashed the Scots 9-3 at Wembley to clinch the British Championship in 1961. Jimmy Greaves scored a hat-trick in England's biggest win against the 'auld enemy'. Wembley had never seen as many goals in a single match.

British Championship
Jimmy Greaves scoring England's third goal as the team went on to beat Scotland 9-3 at Wembley 15.04.1961

GREAT

A special match was played in Glasgow to mark the Scottish FA's Centenary in '73 and England's 5-0 winning margin was the best since 1888. It was Bobby Moore's hundredth appearance for England and the visitors scored three times in the first 15 minutes on a Hampden Park pitch partly covered by snow. Scotland made valiant attempts to get back into the match, but the English defence showed no mercy.

Revie had replaced Ramsey as England's manager by the time the teams clashed again in the British Championship at Wembley in '75. England had a great start, **Gerry Francis rocketing a 25-yarder into the top corner after just four minutes**. Two minutes later Kevin Keegan crossed for **Kevin Beattie to power in a header** and the Scots were floundering' although the final scoreline of 5-1 may have flattered the home side a little.

The two countries didn't meet in the finals of a major tournament until a magical Saturday afternoon during Euro '96. **Gary Neville curled in a cross, Alan Shearer headed past Goram and the reaction from the England fans was ear-splitting.** Two minutes after David Seaman had saved McAllister's penalty, **Paul Gascoigne flicked the ball over Hendry with his left foot and buried a half-volley with his right for a delightful second goal**.

The great rivals haven't met since the Euro 2000 qualifying play-off. England won the away leg of the much-hyped 'Battle of Britain' with a Paul Scholes brace. Scotland made it a close call by ending the second leg 1-0 at Wembley.

ENGLAND WON THE AWAY LEG OF THE MUCH-HYPED 'BATTLE OF BRITAIN'

RIVAL

Euro' 2000 Qualifer England v Scotland Wembley - London Scotland's Don Hutchison rises above the England defence to head his side's goal. 17.11.1999

GUESS WHO

CLUB SIDE IS MANCHESTER UNITED

FIRST NAME HAS FIVE LETTERS

SECOND NAME HAS SIX LETTERS

FIRST NAME STARTS WITH W

SECOND NAME STARTS WITH R

PLAYS AS A STRIKER

Answer:

Answer: Wayne Rooney.

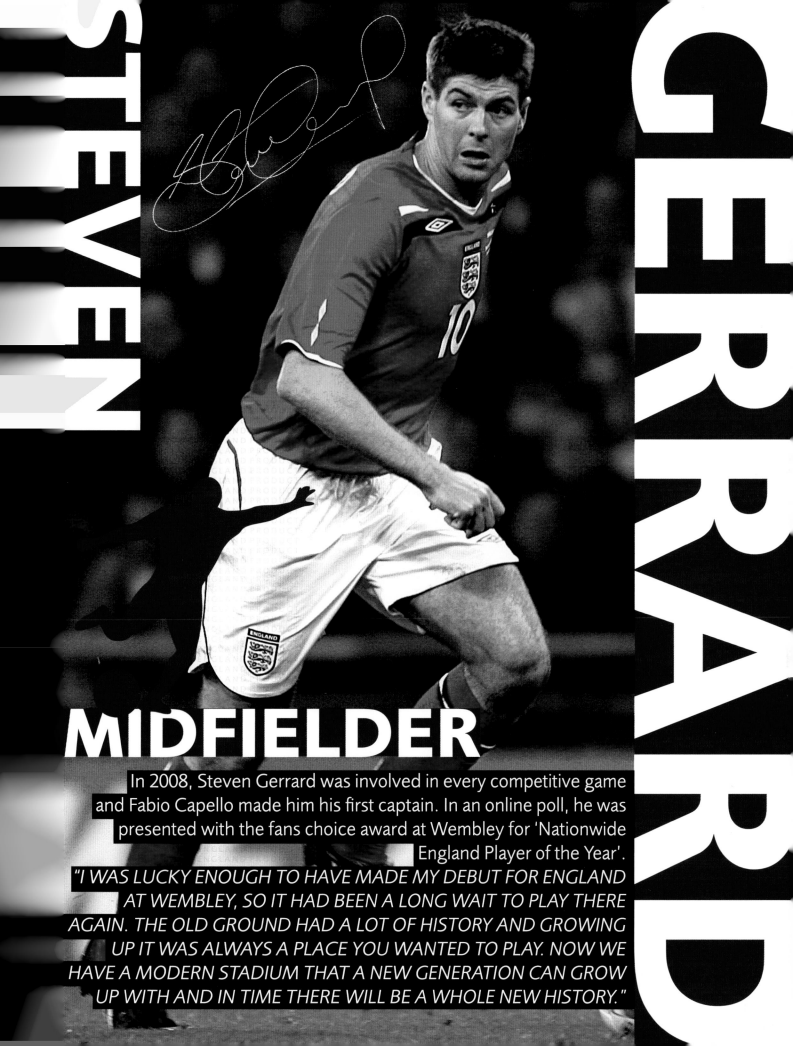

STEVEN

GERRARD

MIDFIELDER

In 2008, Steven Gerrard was involved in every competitive game and Fabio Capello made him his first captain. In an online poll, he was presented with the fans choice award at Wembley for 'Nationwide England Player of the Year'.

"I WAS LUCKY ENOUGH TO HAVE MADE MY DEBUT FOR ENGLAND AT WEMBLEY, SO IT HAD BEEN A LONG WAIT TO PLAY THERE AGAIN. THE OLD GROUND HAD A LOT OF HISTORY AND GROWING UP IT WAS ALWAYS A PLACE YOU WANTED TO PLAY. NOW WE HAVE A MODERN STADIUM THAT A NEW GENERATION CAN GROW UP WITH AND IN TIME THERE WILL BE A WHOLE NEW HISTORY."

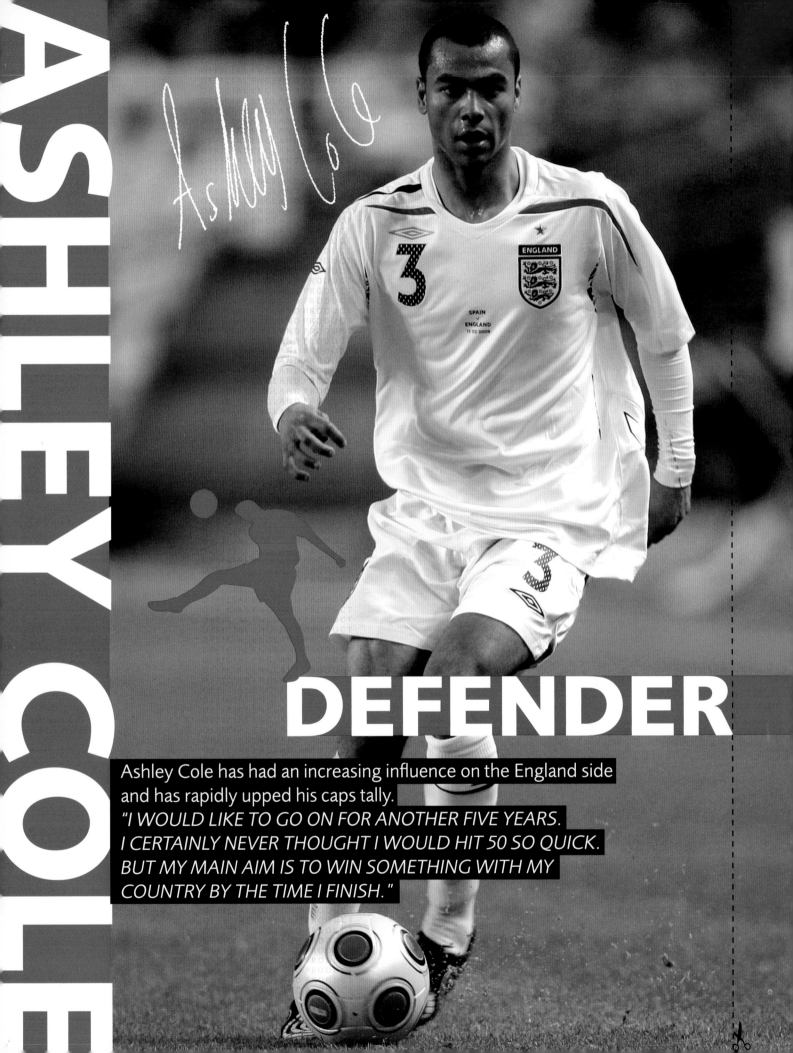

ASHLEY COLE

Ashley Cole

DEFENDER

Ashley Cole has had an increasing influence on the England side and has rapidly upped his caps tally.

"I WOULD LIKE TO GO ON FOR ANOTHER FIVE YEARS. I CERTAINLY NEVER THOUGHT I WOULD HIT 50 SO QUICK. BUT MY MAIN AIM IS TO WIN SOMETHING WITH MY COUNTRY BY THE TIME I FINISH."

TRUE

ARE THE FOLLOWING STATEMENTS ABOUT ENGLAND AND THE PLAYERS TRUE OR FALSE?

Rio Ferdinand made his England debut aged 17 years old. True False

David Beckham was part of the Euro 1996 squad. True False

Paul Robinson made his international debut against Australia. True False

Stewart Downing is the most capped player in the current squad. True False

Frank Lampard, Ashley Cole and Peter Crouch all play for Chelsea. True False

Wayne Rooney made his England debut against Australia. True False

The 2008 European Championship was held in Russia. True False

Phil Jagielka has played for England. True False

Jermaine Jenas started his career at Leicester City. True False

Emile Heskey, Gareth Barry and Ashley Young all play for Aston Villa. True False

FALSE

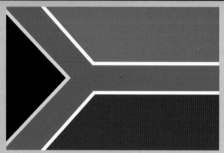

South Africa's National flag

GREEN POINT (CAPE TOWN)

This new stadium with a capacity of 70,000 is a stone's throw from the ocean and the mountains of Cape Town.

8 matches, including a semi-final

DURBAN

Durban has a long footballing history, the first league having been started in one of its provinces. The new stadium, holding 70,000, includes two large archways which will span the roof.

7 matches, including a semi-final

ELLIS PARK (JOHANNESBURG)

Ellis Park was first built in 1928, rebuilt in 1982 and has now undergone an upgrade. The stadium with a 61,000 capacity has been used for the Rugby World Cup and is the home ground of Orlando Pirates.

7 matches, including a quarter-final

SOCCER CITY (JOHANNESBURG)

Soccer City, which hosted the first Nelson Mandela rally after his release, is now the home of football in South Africa. The stadium with a 94,700 capacity has a unique design, with the outer part resembling an African pot.

8 matches, including the Final

FREE STATE

This stadium in Mangaung/ Bloemfontein has hosted matches in the CAF Africa Cup of Nations and the Rugby World Cup. A costly upgrade will increase the capacity to 48,000.

6 matches, including one in the Round of 16

PORT ELIZABETH

Despite not having a team in the Premier League, this is a city which is passionate about football. A new stadium holding 48,000 is being built on the North End Lake, making it an idyllic setting for match days. The three-tier design includes two rings of skyboxes.

8 matches, including the match for Third Place

RLD CUP AFRICA

11 JUNE 2010　TO　11 JULY 2010

LOFTUS VERSFELD

Loftus Versfeld, often just 'Loftus', in the heart of Tshwane/Pretoria will be upgraded to bring it to a 50,000 capacity. The site was first used for sport in 1903, has hosted CAF Africa Cup of Nations and Rugby World Cup matches and is now home to Mamelodi Sundowns.

6 matches, including one in the Round of 16

PETER MOKABA

Polokwane's new stadium will be situated in the Peter Mokaba Sports Complex, named after a political activist during apartheid. With its 46,000 capacity it will be a suitable addition to the Limpopo Province, where they have the country's largest number of registered footballers.

4 matches

ROYAL BAFOKENG

The Royal Bafokeng Sports Palace in Rustenburg is named after the Bafokeng people who live in the area. The stadium with a 42,000 capacity has hosted many Premier League matches.

6 matches, including one in the Round of 16

MBOMBELA

The new stadium with its rounded rectangular shape and 46,000 capacity is close to game parks, allowing fans to see wildlife on rest days.

4 matches

Work continues on Soccer City in Johannesburg, South Africa, which will host both the opening and final matches of the 2010 World Cup 20.02.2009

The 2010 World Cup, the 19th in history, will be played in South Africa from 11 June to 11 July. It will be the first time that the tournament has been hosted by a country in the Confederation of African Football.

Africa was chosen as part of a policy to rotate the event between confederations. Five countries placed bids and South Africa's right to host the World Cup was announced in Zurich on 15 May 2004.

As the host country, South Africa automatically qualifies for the 2010 Finals. But South Africa is actually the first host since 1934 to participate in qualifiers, because they also serve as the qualifying competition for the 2010 African Cup of Nations, for which South Africa needs to qualify separately.

The draw for the World Cup Finals will take place at the Cape Town International Convention Centre on 4 December 2009.

The official World Cup mascot is Zakumi, a leopard with green hair. His name comes from 'ZA', the international abbreviation for South Africa and 'kumi', a word that means 'ten' in various African languages.

It has only been 15 years since South Africa returned from almost three decades of apartheid-enforced isolation on the football scene. During that period the country's national team, Bafana Bafana ('The Boys'), has qualified for two World Cup Finals and also won the CAF Africa Cup of Nations.

Joel Santana is the 15th coach to take charge of the South African side in as many years. He started the job in May 2008. The 59-year-old Brazilian will have the task of reviving the country's struggling national team ahead of the 2010 World Cup.

Prior to South Africa's suspension, they had played just 22 internationals, winning 16 of them. South Africa's best footballers now play in the top leagues of the world, including those in England, Belgium, Germany, Greece, Holland, Russia and Switzerland.

205 countries entered the 2010 World Cup and 32 of them will line up in the Finals. There will be 13 from Europe, 6 from Africa, 4 (or 5) from Asia, 3 (or 4) from CONCACAF*, 1 (or 0) from Oceania and 4 (or five) from South America.

*Includes North and Central America and the Caribbean

England were drawn in European Qualifying Group 6 and started the campaign with five wins in five matches. Fabio Capello's team beat Andorra 2-0 (away), Croatia 4-1 (away), Kazakhstan 5-1 (home), Belarus 3-1 (away). and Ukraine 2-1 (home) on 1 April.

SOUTH AFRICAN COACH JOEL SANTANA

FILL IN YOUR CHART AT THE END OF THE GROUP STAGE

GROUP A

TEAM	Pld	W	D	L	GF	GA	GD	Pts

GROUP B

TEAM	Pld	W	D	L	GF	GA	GD	Pts

GROUP C

TEAM	Pld	W	D	L	GF	GA	GD	Pts

GROUP D

TEAM	Pld	W	D	L	GF	GA	GD	Pts

GROUP E

TEAM	Pld	W	D	L	GF	GA	GD	Pts

GROUP F

TEAM	Pld	W	D	L	GF	GA	GD	Pts

GROUP G

TEAM	Pld	W	D	L	GF	GA	GD	Pts

GROUP H

TEAM	Pld	W	D	L	GF	GA	GD	Pts

ROUND OF 16

QUARTER-FINALS

27 June - Johannesburg

27 June - Bloemfontein

3 July - Cape Town

29 June - Pretoria

29 June - Cape Town

3 July - Johannesburg

26 June - Port Elizabeth

26 June - Rustenburg

2 July - Johannesburg

28 June - Durban

2 July - Port Elizabeth

28 June - Johannesburg

STAGE

WORLD CUP 2010

SEMI-FINALS

7 July - Durban

6 July - Cape Town

FINAL

11 July - Johannesburg

THIRD PLACE

10 July - Port Elizabeth

2010